MW01113774

2.6 to ONE : Why You MUST *shrink* to GROW

Grace Roberts

2.6 to One:

Why You Must shrink to GROW

Copyright Notice

2.6 to One: Why You Must shrink to GROW

Copyright ©2017 Grace Roberts

Published by Krystal Klear Communications, L.L.C.

PRINTED IN THE UNITED STATES OF AMERICA

All rights reserved, including the right to reproduce this book or portion thereof in any form whatsoever. No part of this book may be reproduced or transmitted in any form without written consent from the author.

.

ISBN - 10: 1976192811

ISBN - 13: 978-1976192814

DEDICATION

This book is dedicated to my family, who helped shape the woman I am.

I thank God for choosing you for my journey.

My mother, who gave birth to me after the doctors warned you of being a high risk. Thank you for teaching me how to pray even before I was able to read. Thank you for teaching me to read at 2 ½ years old. I love you. Sorry about the red bulbs. Miss your smile and laughter.

My daddy, beyond your abrasiveness and calloused exterior, God revealed your heart and the core of who you really were. Although daddy, you told me, "I didn't know how to raise no daughters," You were a good provider.

I knew you loved me. You so loved your children.

I really miss those Sunday dinners. You are my hero. I miss you daddy.

My "baby" sis, Kim (My Carmelita), I had no idea I would be writing…sharing my story—my life. God knew. Losing you was the greatest loss and the greatest pain I have ever experienced. You are my inspiration.

I believe you would be proud I am finally writing this. I love you.

I miss you so.

ACKNOWLEDGMENTS

I would like to take a moment to acknowledge those who have been a huge part of this journey:

Matilda Hawkins, "The Queen Bee"

I am so blessed to have you in my life. You are filled with much wisdom and God's Light truly shines in you. Proverbs 31:28 reads, Her children arise up, and call her blessed; her husband also, and he praiseth her. (KJV)

You are a true example of God's love personified. I thank you for your love, and especially your prayers, QBII.

My business coach and friend, DeLores Pressley, who does everything in Excellence. Thank you for sharing your gifts & blessings with the World. God answers Prayers.

The Amazing Visionary Audra T. Jones, thank you for the opportunity.

My dearest J…thank you for your continued support, wisdom and encouragement.

My Lord & Savior, Jesus Christ, thank you for your choice… the ultimate choice.

FOREWORD

By Audra T. Jones, M.B.A

It has been an honor and a pleasure to journey this road with such a dynamic group of women! We started with the goal of inspiring and influencing others with a transparent and open narrative of our individual passions and the journey we took to discovery. We have accomplished that and so much more with our willingness to share our stories. Yes, we all have a story to tell- the difference is whether we choose to actually TELL IT!

Thank you Deb, Lesia, Jacquie, Tami, Teresa and Grace for trusting and believing in my vision to help inspire, educate and influence others to seek their passion while enjoying the journey! We are living out God's intentional abundance for us and I look forward to greater heights in all aspects of your lives.

I believe this collection of vignettes will serve as a useful tool to encourage people to embrace their past and catapult their efforts and experiences to discovering their future.

The pain, the discovery, and the emergence of purpose and passion will intrigue you and stir your soul to empowerment.

Peace and Blessings,

Audra T. Jones
"The Krystal Klear Specialist"

TABLE OF CONTENTS

01

CHAPTER

01

2.6 TO ONE: WHY YOU MUST *SHRINK* TO GROW

...you are built, not to shrink down to less,
but to blossom into more...
--Oprah Winfrey

Grace Roberts

2.6 to ONE: Why You Must *shrink* to GROW

You gon' die tonight b*&^@!" What? I thought. I could not believe what was happening. Is this it? Lord, am I going to die? Like this? Barely an adult, I have not even made an impact in life. This can't be happening. These thoughts ran through my mind and my heart raced, as he came over to the sofa and straddled me on the sofa, I said, "No Joe, don't! Stop! As he wrapped his hands around my neck and began to choke me...consciousness fading. "Lord, I haven't begun to live. Lord, why? Why? At least I know I'm going to heaven, just didn't realize it would be so soon." I knew my life had to have more purpose than this.

When I regained consciousness, I thought,"Oh, I'm not dead?" Joe was on the other end of the sofa with his face cupped in his hands, seemingly remorseful that he thought he choked me to death. He even seemed to be crying. When I got up, I yelled hysterically, "What did you do? Look what you did to me!" My face and my neck were in excruciating pain. I walked to the bathroom to examine my face. My face, eyes & neck hurt so badly I could not even cry. I tried. Nothing. I yelled, "I can't even cry," as I looked at the very visible pronounced hand prints on my neck. The whites of my eyes were almost completely red. I tried to cry, again-Nothing. I yelled, Look what you did to me! I am going to call the police. When I returned to the sofa, he apologized. I was in shock. I thought I was in the twilight zone. Still in disbelief, I wondered, "How did I let this happen? How could I get into a relationship with someone who I thought loved me, filled with abuse? How did I get here?

I had no idea what love was, so how could I determine what was and was not love? One thing I did know, this was NOT love. Still, I wondered, "how did I end up here?"

This is one event in my life, where I thought I would shrink beyond return, and retreat. I now realize that in order to fulfill my divine purpose and destiny, I had to shrink, many times throughout my life, to grow into the true destiny God has called for my life. Merriam-Webster.com defines shrink: - intransitive verb, 2a) to contract to less extent or compass, 2d) to lessen in value, 3a) to recoil instinctively (as from something painful or horrible) 3b) to hold oneself back. In retrospect, these times in my life during the "shrinking processes" released my resilience and strength to mold the woman I was to become, living in the purpose on purpose.

Let's go back to where it all began.

I was supposed to be born a summer baby, but I was born in the springtime. I was born 2 lbs., 6 oz., 3 months early. My weight dropped to 1 lb. I was not expected to live. The doctors' did not think I would make it. The outcome did not seem to be in my favor. 2 lbs., 6 oz., to 1 lb. It really didn't seem it would end well for me, no happy ending for my family. I remained incubated for many months. 2.6 to 1? How? But God! I'm sure my parents' daily visits and prayers made all the difference as well. Instinctively, my daddy called me, "Hope". So the journey of the "daddy's girl" began.

Merriam-Webster.com defines hope: intransitive verb- to desire with expectation of obtainment or fulfillment; to expect with confidence; a feeling of expectation and desire for a certain thing to happen. MLA

Ironically, I was truly a "daddy's girl." I always wanted daddy's approval. Seeking his approval in everything, from grades and education to relationships to career choices, daddy's opinion mattered more than anyone in the world. I desired to be stellar in my dad's sight.

He was a multi-faceted man from the South who migrated to the North. Daddy was a proud man. He was a compassionate man. He was not a subservient man, by no stretch of imagination. He left the South because he could not stand the way the black men were treated, and he was not going to be treated as such. A self-taught son of a sharecropper, he was a product of extreme poverty and would often speak of giving his shoes to his brother, and he would go to school with none. Because his clothing was riddled with holes, he would forego the recess with the other kids, and remain against the wall, so the other kids could not taunt him about the holes in his clothing. He remained a southern boy at heart, although the residue of the Jim Crow era and the extreme abuse from his father left him hardened with a tough callous shell. I learned of one instance of abuse, when he was a young boy, when he spoke up to his father, he was removed from the house then forced to sleep under their house, with the rodents and animals. Because of these dire actions, influences and abuses during his youth, as an adult, he overindulged in alcohol to cope with many of the pains, hurts and trauma of his past. I can only imagine the level of hurt & humiliation this caused for my dad.

My dad was an avid reader and was up at the crack of dawn, daily, in the news, reading the paper and he always promoted the importance of education. Given the opportunity, I believe my dad would have graduated college and perhaps become a college professor. His education was interrupted, as he served in the U.S. Army. When he returned home, he finished school. He loved to learn and teach and he always told us there is always opportunity to learn in everything we do. He was a structured supervisor with an amazing work ethic, and was well respected and highly regarded in his industry. Even when he retired, he was invited to return, and he did, he chose to return on a part-time basis. Yet it was the hurts and pains of his past that consumed him, and the alcohol was the tool he used to cope, and the tool to help him raise his children. I painfully watched my dad attempt to mask his pain.

As I transitioned from a child into adolescence, as with most children, my life was filled with a myriad of emotions and uncertainty. My dad projected his harsh criticisms, humiliations and verbal attacks on me. It did not matter where or when the abuse took place. He had no filter and I happened to be the one to whom he directed the rants. Whether I was outside with friends, at our neighbor's home, or even in front of our guests, I became the object of my father's most embarrassing alcoholic rage and ridicule. "You will never amount to anything!" was most commonly directed toward me as I was growing up. Growing up in such a household was more stressful than most. When daddy was not drinking, I was his hero and he spoke loving words of affirmation. However, my father was more often inebriated than not early on. It was quite the contrast as he began to drink. The firestorm of words began.

He told me as a young girl, to always speak my mind. Yet when I spoke my mind to him, as he told me to, he cussed me out. This is **not** a bashing of my father, by no means. It is simply to explain my journey and insight into the life of my father. One moment I was hailed as his hero, the next, I was told, "You're going to be in jail before you're 16, before you're 18." I was not a bad kid. Of course, like most kids, a little mouthy at times. My dad always told me to speak my mind, so when I did and it conflicted with his opinions, he cursed me out and told me I was going to jail. Why dad? Simply for speaking my mind, I was admonished. There were times when I thought

I would shrink beyond return, and I wondered, "How could my father love me, but treat me in such a manner?"

I was such an outgoing, strong-willed little girl, opinionated, even seemingly defiant at times. As I was growing up, of course, I was very inquisitive and I thought my parents didn't understand me." I remember thinking, "Maybe I was adopted, because these "folks" could not be my parents, acting as they did." I remember when I was around 5 or 6 years old, we had a vacuum cleaner, which was missing a small knob, and it was inoperable without it. I knew nothing about the cleaner nor the missing knob, but I was blamed for it. I remember both of my parents yelling at me as I sat in the middle of the kitchen floor, and my dad cursing at me for this. They told me I lost it and needed to find it. I cried incessantly. I told them I had no idea, but they did not listen. My dad made me dump the trash in the middle of the kitchen floor and I had to search through the trash for this knob, which I knew nothing of. I remember them yelling over me as I sifted through the disgustingly smelly garbage. I did not find the knob of course, after hours of exhausting myself, all the while I am telling them through my tears, I did not lose it. I returned to the living room, sat on the floor to watch T.V. and my parents followed me and resumed yelling and cursing at me about this. I cried until I thought my tear ducts were depleted of any tears, my head began to hurt and when I tried to get up, I could not move my legs. I froze in that moment and it seemed I was having an out of body experience. I could not move my legs, and I began to shout back at my parents, **" I can't move my legs!"** I needed their help, as I pleaded with them. Again, they did not believe me. I yelled repeatedly. "This could not get any worse," I thought. I couldn't get away from the incessant yelling and screaming at me and the two people I needed most, would not come to my rescue and they did not believe me. Finally after an hour or so, after they left the room, as I was drifting off, I was able to move. That had never happened to me before and has never happened since.

In the midst of my dad's constant ongoing verbal abuse I could not fathom how he could love me as his daughter, as his actions spoke the opposite. I never knew what any given day would bring. The continual barrage of verbal abuse was commonplace in my home. Anyone who knew our family, knew that my dad could erupt in any moment, anytime, anywhere. This was anything but a traditional home life. We witnessed constant conflict in our home. If it were not mom & dad yelling and arguing, it would be dad and/or mom yelling at me or mom vs daughter, dad vs daughter. It was often a hostile environment. This existence left much to be desired. As far as my parents' relationship, I knew if that was what marriage was, I certainly wanted NO part of it. This had been my way of life and I was tired and drained mentally, physically and emotionally. I most often felt I had no one. I sought the Lord. "Someone had to be on my side, if I was going through "hell" on earth," I thought. I had an innate sense of God's presence in my life, so I began to pray. Unbeknownst to me at the time, God's hand was and had always been on me. Even in my darkest times, he was there.

As I prepared to graduate from high school, I was uncertain of my immediate future. "Am I going to college or join the armed forces?" I questioned. While we were in school, daddy had a hefty college fund for me & my sister. However, a business deal w/ a "supposed" friend & colleague went sour, down the tubes and so did our college fund. Daddy did ask us if he could invest our college fund w/ possible financial gain/loss for our family. Of course, we said, "Yes." I decided to take the Armed Services Vocational Aptitude Battery (ASVAB). My dad took me to the Federal building for all day testing. I tested quite well, so I was on my way to the Air Force. I thought my path was set. I would go to the Air Force, have the military pay for my college education, and then I would retire from the Air Force. I received my orders, and it was time to get sworn in, before graduation. My recruiter, Sgt. Wells was the most patient helpful recruiter and my dad seemed to be pleased with my decision, almost… It was swearing in time. Sgt. Wells came to pick me up for my swearing in. All of a sudden, I felt a cramp in my stomach. I decided I could not be sworn in. Sgt. Wells waited, as my father yelled for me to go to my swearing-in ceremony. I was going to get sworn in alone. Neither of my parents would be going with me and by this time I had decided I was not going to the Air Force. I did not wish to leave my family, and reluctant, even of the thought of being away from home. Ironically, the person who seemed to treat me the worst, was the person I hated to leave the most and he was not pleased about my "stomach ache." He yelled a few expletives up the stairs, in the attempt to get me down stairs and out the door. No, I did not have a stomachache and wasn't ready to launch. Why was I not ready to leave home? Did I allow fear to immobilize me? Why such apprehension? Was it the uncertainty of my future? The thought of me leaving made me prematurely "homesick." "What was my next step?" I had no idea. God knew.

After high school, I prepared to attend a local university. On my birthday, I received the acceptance letter. I was so excited. My family and I toured the campus and housing. I was ready to go. I had it mapped out. After all, I "knew" what my plans were for my life.

Jeremiah 29:11 For I know the thoughts that I think toward you, saith the LORD, thoughts of peace, and not of evil, to give you an expected end. KJV .

"For I know the plans I have for you," declares the LORD, "plans to prosper you and not to harm you, plans to give you hope and a future. NIV Bible.

Of course, I had no idea what was to come. God did. Once we returned home, I completed and submitted my financial aid paperwork. I was already imagining college life. parties, boys, dorms, cramming, boys exams, Greek life. As I was preparing to say farewell to my friends and family, I received news from the financial aid office. I would not be receiving ANY financial assistance, as my father's income exceeded the income guidelines. That was his money, not mine. He was not giving me ANY money, so why should his money matter to me. I was discouraged and disappointed. Well, that was the end of my college aspirations at the time. My dad said, "I guess you could get a job." That's just what I did. But, I knew my path was not as my dad's, nor what my dad wanted for me at the time. Of course, God knew.

I was a smart girl academically, but I was a fragmented young woman. If I was so smart, why had I not received full scholarship offers to attend the college or university of my choice? "Why was I not on my way to being a president of a university or a corporation," I wondered. God knew. Perhaps I had bought into what my father said to me all those years. Had I subconsciously begun to believe what daddy and other family members said to me? "After all, if he said it, it must be truth, right?" Had I fallen into a spirit of mediocrity and complacency?

God's hand was always upon me and hedge of protection always around me. God was my Heavenly Father, and he was everything I needed. Although I grew up in my dad's household, God was to be my first love/parent/confidant/protector.

The father-daughter dynamic is so important in a girl's life. It is crucial for a girl's development and well being. The relationship between a girl and her father formulates her standards and expectations of men. Her father is the first example of what a man is. I had far from the idealistic upbringing. No, I never went to a daddy/daughter dance. Daddy didn't take me. No, daddy never bought flowers for his daughters' and he never took me on my first daddy/daughter date. Sadly, I never experienced this. I did not have my father impart and pour affirmation into my spirit. Daddy did not esteem his daughters, as I longed for. Although I did not have the "perfect" relationship with my father, I was still daddy's girl, and longed for his love and approval. It wasn't until I was a young woman, that I realized he could only give what he had and knew how to give. As much as I wanted the idealistic daddy-daughter relationship, my father could not give me something he did not possess. Daddy possessed a strong work ethic, he was very intelligent, great promoter of education, a sense of humor and was a good provider. I really wished he would have been more hands on raising us.

Along the way, I met and began to date a young man named Joe. I told my dad all about him. My dad never really liked anyone I dated, as he felt I was dating beneath my privilege. When my dad met him, he really didn't say much. He simply observed, and since I was excited about it, he "tolerated" the relationship. My dad and I would have conversations about Joe. When he would visit, my dad deduced that there was something not quite right about him. Of course, I tried to explain to my dad, since I was 18-years old, and knew everything. I told my dad, Joe was misunderstood. Yet it was only a matter of time before I began to experience abuse, from Joe. It started with verbal, emotional and graduated to physical violence and abuse. My father warned me, "If his family doesn't want to have anything to do with him, there must be something wrong." Since I believed that daddy couldn't possibly love me as I should be loved, how could he possibly know about Joe. I ignored my dad's warning.

During this on/off relationship, it became clear what I did not want in a relationship, and more importantly what love was NOT. I ended the relationship, however, when his grandmother fell ill, I returned to the relationship, to support him. I tried to help him, so I thought. I was trying to be the "savior". His grandmother passed. After she died, the relationship continued to disintegrate. I soon realized I should not have gotten back with Joe, and now I was trying to figure out how to get out of the relationship permanently. I could not dare tell my father anything, I feared he would ridicule and crucify me about staying in the relationship. "I had to get out, but how?" This would be one of the worst times in my life where I thought I would "shrink" to my demise.

Joe would spend time with his family, but had no stable home life. His grandmother coddled him through his life, and when she died none of his family allowed him to live with them. I later realized Joe was homeless. I tried to help him find places to live, to no avail. I could find temporary fixes for him, but he had no initiative to do anything beyond my assistance.

Once we were visiting friends, and they offered their sofa for a week. We decided to stay with them. My mother lent her assistance, but she encouraged me to return home. She reassured me that I had support of family, but I should go home. It would be in my best interest to go home. "He was an adult, she said, "and he would figure it out on his own." I chose to stay.

By this time, I was mentally, physically & emotionally tapped out, and what my parents reiterated to me rushed me like a ton of bricks. I told Joe I was leaving, but I would still help him. He was in total disagreement with me. He pleaded with me to stay, but I insisted, I was going home the next day. When it was time to go to sleep, Joe wanted to have sex. He attempted to climb on top of me. I exclaimed, "No, I am not having sex with you!" Enraged, he aggressively told me, "If you don't give it to me, I will take it!" I told him to stop, several times, as he violently ripped my panties off of me. This bastard violated me! He raped me. No means No! NO meant NO. He raped me. I layed there helpless, defenseless, lifeless. I cried myself to sleep. I still have a faint scar on my leg where he tore my undergarment off of me, as a reminder. I never reported this to the police. I wondered, "Who would believe I was raped by my "*boyfriend*"?"

I began to retreat. I began to withdraw. Joe was apologetic the next day, but his apology meant nothing to me. How could I tell anyone about this? Who would believe me? I prayed and cried until I was all cried out. I sought God through the pain, guilt and embarrassment, yet, I still felt so ashamed. I think I was in shock. The "man" I thought loved me, did the unthinkable to me. How? Why? Again, I didn't understand, but some small light inside of me led me to know that I would be fine, no matter what. Even through this, God's hand was always upon me. The question remained…why had I not yet left this relationship?

I was afraid of what our friends would say if they found out. They were in the next room, and maybe they wouldn't believe me either. Maybe Joe would lie about the rape, and no one else would believe me. I allowed fear to cripple my better judgement? At some point, I felt I succumbed to the relationship and I felt stuck, at the point of no return. This "shrinking" episode would be the greatest to date. If I thought I would drown in anything, this would be it. How did I end up in this calamity of a relationship? I was smarter than this. Several months later he attempted to kill me. I could have lost my life at the hands of this man. Of course, I asked how? Why? How could or would I know what love truly was, when I had never experienced a healthy example of such a love? It wasn't until I surrendered to the total love of God and purposed in my heart, his sacrificial, love beyond feelings, beyond emotions. This love was available to me all along. God's Agape love forever changed my life. The Agape love of God is selfless, unconditional, beyond circumstances, beyond fault and judgment.

I Corinthians 13:4-7 probably best describes the agape love of God. KJV- 7) Beareth all things, believeth all things, hopeth all things, endureth all things. NIV- 7) It always protects, always trusts, always hopes, always perseveres.

My relationship with my father had reached a new plateau. No longer was he the abrasive, verbally abusive dad. As I grew, so did my dad. As I spent more time with him, I began to see a less abrasive, softer side of him. I prayed for him and his well being. The more time I spent with him, God gave me a renewed heart and new love for my father. I began to see him as God saw him. He was precious to God, and was a masterpiece to him. In the words of Dr. Seuss' in "The Grinch who Stole Christmas," …And what happened then? Well...in

Whoville they say, That the Grinch's small heart Grew three sizes that day! (Dr. Seuss-How the Grinch Stole Christmas, 1966) The Grinch was one of my favorites growing up, and as a little girl, in my mind, there was a strong similarity, between daddy and the Grinch. Not to liken either to the Grinch, but all of those years now… all of the "shrinking" in our relationship was for this very moment. I believe during this time both of our hearts grew. The growth in my heart and spirit was illuminated; I fell in love with my daddy! Anew! It was as if the slate was blank. God gave us a new start. Halleluiah!

Merriam-Webster.com defines grow: intransitive verb 1a) to spring up and develop to maturity 1c) to assume some relation through or as if through a process of natural growth 2b) to have an increasing influence

"Grow." Merriam-Webster.com. Merriam-Webster, n.d. Web. 6 Mar. 2017.

Dictionary.com defines grow: (v)
to arise or issue as a natural development from an original happening, circumstance, or source:

"grow". Dictionary.com Unabridged. Random House, Inc. 7 Mar. 2017.
<Dictionary.com http://www.dictionary.com/browse/grow>.

My dad had not been well for quite some time. I knew something was wrong, but dad was one who kept it to himself. As most men, he was not big on going to the doctor either. The year before dad died, I decided to host Thanksgiving dinner at my home. Even my dad, who hardly went anywhere, came with his wife. Family speaks to the fiber of who I am and has always been so important to me. Dad didn't go out often, so I was elated that he decided to come. He didn't stay long, and I knew something else was wrong, but he seldom complained. Weeks later I decided to fast on his behalf for 7 days, with no food or drink, only H2O. I didn't know then, but my daddy would be gone in less than 6 months.

The prognosis came early the next year. We went to the hospital, with hopes of surgery for my dad to correct any issues, however, that was not the case. The doctor gave us the prognosis, dad had cancer and it was too far-gone to do anything. Daddy had between two to six months to live, we were told. I went numb. It seemed like time stopped. I remember my dad's wife & I sitting in the hospital cafeteria in silence. I was in denial. Perhaps God would heal him and all would be well, I wished. Tears streamed down my face. I could not believe my daddy was not going to be around to celebrate our birthdays, milestones. He would not be around to walk me down the aisle. I couldn't believe there would be no more Sunday dinners at dad's. My brother, sister & I would call each other to see what time we would arrive at dad's for dinner. My dad was great cook. He was a southern boy, and I remember growing up with a garden full of fresh veggies, from greens to green beans to peppers to onions, tomatoes, cabbage and he would pick them straight from the garden to the table. He even planted fresh herbs. How I cherish those memories.

As we talked with daddy, he opted for surgery, but I told him that would only be a temporary fix, there was no permanent cure. Between dad's wife and myself, there was always someone with him at the hospital. Dad was not the easiest patient, and there were times the nursing staff left his room, not wanting to deal with the difficult patient known as my daddy. As his health declined, he was unable to use the bathroom on his own anymore, and the nurses had to lift him from the bed to the commode. Often, the nurses' staff would be very slow to respond. Sometime he would get no response at all. Of course, I am my father's daughter and I would seek out the staff for him. At one point, after getting no assistance from the hospital staff, I recall searching the closets up and down the hall, for chux pads for my dad. Dad had to use the bathroom, and he was tired of "holding" it in until someone came to help him. I told him to "do his business", do what he needed to do, and I would change him. I know that had to be most humbling for him to have his daughter, see him in this condition, and to have to have her change his chux pads; this was truly humbling for my dad, I'm sure. No one else will care enough to take care of your family as well as you can, I truly believed. So between myself and his wife, one of us was always there with him. Whenever he needed to use the "chux" to relieve himself, I reassured him, "I got you, daddy." He knew we were there to be sure he would receive the best care.

Daddy wanted to spend his last days at his home. We would not have had it any other way. Things were different when he returned home, but we tried to create as much normalcy as possible. He returned home to a hospital bed, not his bed he shared with his wife. He was also to be placed in another bedroom, not his. We wanted him to be as comfortable as possible. It was all about daddy. Whatever he wanted, we got it for him. Daddy wanted catfish. I went to the market to get the fish, freshly flown in 3x/week. Got it. Daddy loved potatoes and onions. My sister came and prepared it for him. Daddy craved fried green tomatoes. We made sure he had all that he wanted. Thinking back to stories of him not having shoes as a child, and having to walk to school barefoot, I offered to wash his rough, weathered feet. He did not like anyone touching his feet and he was resistant. He said, "No! Don't touch my feet." As days passed, I asked a few more times, and he finally said, "Yes." Heck, I had this amazing peppermint lotion and peppermint body wash and he had to try it. With a spirit of servitude, I placed his feet in the foot spa. He didn't say a word. I soaked his feet, exfoliated them, and then washed them. He remained quiet. I wonder what his thoughts were? Probably, "This damn girl will worry me to death, until I say yes." I then gently washed and dried his feet, topping off with lotion and massaging my dad's feet. I never thought in a million years, I would touch my daddy's feet. Afterward, I put his footies back on his feet, and placed them back under his covers. I made sure he was comfortable; I kissed him and thanked him for allowing me to serve him. As he drifted off to sleep, I whispered, "I love you daddy."

Daddy, I thank God for you. I thank God for the man you were, which helped me become the woman I am, and helped define me and my purpose. I miss our conversations, and I miss coming over for dinner on Sunday. I thank you for the dimple in my left cheek, and I thank you for passing along the spirit of giving, generosity and philanthropy to me. You were so selfless. I thank you for giving me a selfless heart for people and inherently giving me the best of you. I so often reflect on our conversations, and I often think of advice you gave me. I thank you for the desire to learn and dream big. Although you were tough and we didn't always agree, thank you for allowing me to GROW into my purpose. I miss those greens! Mine are almost as good as yours… Love, your daughter, "Hopey"

"Heavenly Father, I humbly come before you, always asking and thanking you for your understanding, your vision, and your wisdom, Lord. I thank you for my family, my father, and most importantly, YOU. Your protection, your hand has always covered me, even when I was unaware. Thank you for being all that I need in every circumstance on every level. You have always been there. I thank you for your agape love, I thank you for being my first love, my provider, my father/mother and everything I have ever needed in between. Lord, I thank you for the times in my life when I felt I was shrinking in despair, being reduced even to the point of insignificance beyond return, yet these instances were designed to promote and foster my strength and growth. Thank you for never leaving nor changing, thank you for your ever presence. Thank you for your word of instruction, as I strive toward excellence. You ARE excellent! Thank you for creating me in your image. Lord, I thank you for your peace beyond understanding, and I will be careful to give you all the Praise, Power, Honor & Glory, In Jesus' name, AMEN.

Dr. George Fraser, Founder/CEO FraserNet once told me, "Stay the course." I shall. I encourage you to do the same.

ABOUT THE AUTHOR

As Director of Community Affairs for Rubber City Radio's WNWV-107.3FM, Grace Roberts is dedicated to putting the spotlight on grassroots efforts in Northeast Ohio that work to serve community, including military veterans and their families. The host, speaker and newly penned author's passion is service, especially to empower the disenfranchised. Grace "On The Go", showcases Cleveland's commitment to service through organizations like Malachi House, Maltz Museum of Jewish Heritage, NASA Glenn Research Center and United Cerebral Palsy of Greater Cleveland to name a few.

As on-air host with Radio One Cleveland, she also hosted/produced community affairs and entertainment programs, Urban Spotlight & Access Cleveland and was "First Lady of Mid-days" on Praise 1300.

Some notable interviews are Dr. Alex Johnson, President of Cuyahoga Community College; Former U.S. Secretary of Education, Arne Duncan; Activist Yolanda King; Olympic Figure Skater, Scott Hamilton, Stedman Graham and President Barack H. Obama. Grace took 2nd place in Duffy Liturgical Dance Ensemble's "Dancing" w/ the Stars, Celebrity Contest. In 2016, she co-hosted a new game show, "Mox Nix," meaning, "Makes no difference," 'Cause everybody wins!

Grace volunteers and serves with various agencies in Northeast Ohio, as she lives by the mantra, "At your service, how may I serve you?" In 2016, Grace dealt with the untimely passing of her sister and embraces music of the WAVE and God's Word for strength and healing. Wife of a 30-year veteran of the U.S. Military, Grace is a dedicated advocate for veterans. Grace and her family reside in Northeast Ohio.

GRACE ROBERTS

02

CHAPTER

02

GOD PUT A WORD IN MY EAR

AUDRA T. JONES, M.B.A.

GOD PUT A WORD IN MY EAR
PART 1 WHO ARE YOU?

N O, please…please…I do not want to go! Please, I can live with grandma and granddaddy…please don't make me go!"

I recall muttering these words to my parents through tears of anguish as they revealed our family was moving! Moving? Moving? Honestly I could not comprehend what they were saying at the time…as my dad continued to proudly announce that "We were moving to the West Side"

Moving, Moving? What does that mean, we are moving? As a 10-year old child, I could not comprehend living somewhere other than where I was currently living. I was NOT thrilled with the idea of making new friends, getting adjusted to a new school and living in a new house.

As the summer progressed, our family prepared to move from one side of town to the other side of town. My parents were thrilled with the move as they were excited to provide additional avenues for an exceptional learning experience for my sister and I. I, on the other hand was not happy and found very quickly I did not fit in with the rest of the children in the neighborhood.

I did not look like the other children, I did not act like the other children, I did not speak like the other children, I did not learn like the other children…what was going on and how was I ever going to actually FIT IN? I remember thinking and feeling so lost as a 10 year old in a completely NEW environment.

My parents wanted to provide the best exposure, education, living conditions, etc. and that meant CHANGE was inevitable!

Sitting on the playground as a young child at a new school-I felt alone! I was the only African American in my neighborhood and I terribly missed my friends and the life I once knew. As I thought about how I had to make all new friends, I felt a burning desire to press forward and make the best of the situation. I looked around the playground, perused the groups of students playing and decided I had to get up and DO SOMETHING! Just as I was getting up off the ground, one of the little girls was approaching me, saying, "Hi, do you want to come and play with us?"

From that day forward I was determined to make the BEST of the BIG MOVE to Strongsville, Ohio! I became a model student and a model athlete. ....

I now know that at early age I displayed fortitude and passion to excel beyond the norm.

My parents encouraged me to immerse myself in excellence and seek to surround myself with greatness. Looking back now I realize taking my parents' advice was more challenging than I realized. Living as one of the few African-Americans students in a suburban environment forced me to deal with racism at a very early age. How could I surround myself in excellence with racism rearing its ugly head?

I argued, fought and had to defend myself on PLENTY of occasions. Was this the norm, I wondered? Why were so many people so concerned about the color of my skin? At the tender age of 10, I had no idea what racism was, how to deal with, and certainly no idea on how to avoid it.

Racism as defined by Webster's Dictionary: *a belief or doctrine that inherent differences among the various human racial groups determine cultural or individual achievement, usually involving the idea that one's own race is superior and has the right to dominate others or that a particular racial group is inferior to the others.*

How does a child understand the true meaning of racism? Why does a child HAVE to understand the meaning of racism? Thank God for tough skin and the strong support system I had at home. Although others chose to relish in difference, I chose to relish in opportunity and circumstance! I was encouraged to look beyond the ignorance of others. I tried!

My high school years proved to be no different. I was still forced to deal with racism and classism. I thought, as I got older, things would get better. I thought as we matured and experienced life a little more –things would be different. Saddened to say, the cruelty, anger and disrespect continued.

For the majority of my life, I attended predominantly white school systems. Upon high school graduation, I decided to try my hand at an HBCU (historically black college or university). I wanted to keep my options open so

I visited and applied to colleges and universities across the country including HBCU's (historically black college or university). I received academic and athletic scholarships to several notable institutions- I was on my way...RIGHT? Not quite, the colleges I really wanted to attend had not awarded me any scholarships. I had my heart and mind set on attending an HBCU...It was time for a change!

That change would come with my decision to pursue my degree from Hampton University. I decided to attend site unseen; my parents were not very pleased. My parents trusted and supported my decision to attend Hampton University because they saw how passionate I was for a change in my life.

Chasing the Passion-at age 17, I was headed to a very unfamiliar space to spend the next 4 years of life. I understood at a very young age that I needed to spread my wings outside of the suburban life I was accustomed to living. I was ready to take on college life and all that it had to offer.

As I prepared for college, everyone kept asking me "Aren't you scared?" My answer was always the same "I am not sure what I should be scared of"

Transitioning from a predominantly white high school to a predominantly black university was quite an experience for me! Overcoming some of the cultural and social challenges in college contributed to me evolving as an individual. I was intentional about exposing myself to others that were from different backgrounds culturally, socially and politically. Passionate about creating a place in society I chose early on to stand in the space between!

WHO ARE YOU…NO really…WHO ARE YOU…I ask myself that question as I continue to evolve under this landscape called life! Daughter, Sister, Friend, Confidant, Educator, Entrepreneur, Coach, Motivator, Visionary, Mentor.

I lost the true essence of who I was when I got married! I was so committed to the marriage and the process of building a life as one, that I lost the essence of myself. The essence of who you are is based on you! Never let the desire and passion to please someone else become the vain of your existence. Chasing the Passion can come with a price. I learned that paying that price was out of my budget.

No one ever gets married to get divorced but that is exactly what chasing happiness through someone else led to. Alone, scared, embarrassed, these adjectives accurately described my new normal. I had planned my life around being married forever. I remembered thinking…how am I going to survive? What do I tell people? Should I be embarrassed, that he left me? Should I tell the truth? I was evolving yet again! Who was I NOW? I was no longer a wife, a lover, a soul mate, a life-partner. Chasing the passion? I neglected to mention that after 3 years of marriage, my ex-husband decided to leave me.

Now is that something you really want to share with people? Not really, but at some point, I had to share the news, share the story and share the reality of life as a divorcee.

I was a woman trying to find her way in a sea of loneliness and desperation. I was a woman seeking solitude in the superficial things of life. I was a woman embarrassed at the cards I had been delivered and was desperately trying to play the hand I was dealt.

Philippians 3:14

I press toward the mark for the prize of the high calling of God in Christ Jesus

This has become my mantra.

PART 2 WHAT IS YOUR PASSION AND WHY?

What is your PASSION?   Are you working toward that inner sense of peace that helps build you and those around you or are you simply put, existing from day to day?

Passion compels us to make a difference in the world. Passion can come under the auspices of a dream, vision, talent, burden, or calling. There is no right or wrong passion! We each have areas in our personal, social and professional lives that we are passionate about for a variety of reasons. When we pursue those things that we are passionate about we become more focused and driven! When we do NOT pursue those things we are passionate about, we become tired, burned out and less motivated to make a difference.

What are you PASSIONATE about? Are you making a difference and encouraging others to do the same by way of example?

I am passionate about helping others!   As I think back on the jobs, responsibilities, organizations and committees I have served on, most have primarily been centered on helping others. Giving back and helping others is not only a gift but it is an opportunity for personal growth. My trials and tribulations contributed to the passion I have to help others!   I am dedicated to the spirit of servitude and pattern my life, business, and direction upon the principles of such.

I encourage you to dig deep to find what truly drives you! The journey to discovery means accepting the diligence that MUST accompany the process.

Pursuit=Passion!

"It is obvious that we can no more explain a passion to a person who has never experienced it than we can explain light to the blind" -T.S. Elliot

Here are a few things I recognize about my PURSUIT OF PASSION:

- It is not a hobby

- You do it because it makes you happy

- It may not be something tangible

- You press forward REGARDLESS OF CIRCUMSTANCE

- Inspiration may come from unexpected places, people, and things

- BE and STAY invested! (Mentally, Physically, Spiritually, etc.)

- Shut IT ALL OUT! Fully devote to PURSUIT and ELEVATION!

- Can't STOP; Won't STOP!

- Ambitions and Limitless Energy

- Embrace the Journey

3 THE JOURNEY TO DISCOVERY

Serving according to your passion breathes purpose and influence into your life and into the lives of those around you. The journey to discover one' s passion is not often easy. Some people live their entire lives seeking purpose and ultimately their passion.

I know that self-discovery is not always easy! Here are a few questions to help you assess…what is MY PASSION?

The goal of this quick assessment it to identify in a word, concept or brief phrase what captures the essence of your passion. The following questions/statements are designed to elicit and capture your FIRST response, phrase, or thought.

THE JOURNEY TO DISCOVERING YOUR PASSION:

- If I could make one difference in the world today, I would…

- If you were to ask my closet family members and friends, they would say I am passionate about…

- If I could take on something new and knew the probability of failure was zero, I would…

- When it is all said and done, I would like to look back my life and say that I have made a difference about…

- I have a desire to…

- As I look back over my life, I have spent a great deal of time on or with…

- I feel most connected and driven by the following population:

Children	Married	Unemployed	Athletes
Toddlers	Parents	Teen Moms	Military
Young Adults	Elderly	Abused	Veterans
Singles	Divorced	Prisoners	Government
Disabled	Educators	Health Care	Other

Other (please specify):

- I feel strongly about the following issues/causes:

Injustice	Education	Racism	Homosexuality	Mental Health
Poverty	Technology	Religion	Marriage	Politics
Addiction	Healthcare	Diversity	Economy	Other

Other (please specify):

- The most rewarding LIFE experiences have been:

Most rewarding LIFE experience:	Value Added? Why?

- As you think about your hopes, dreams, goals and accomplishments in life, what consistency do you see?

Here are a few questions to help you drive out the passion within:

- What did you dream about when you were young?

- What are the situations that generated the greatest amount of self-confidence and sense of peace?

- When you think about your BEST day, what does that look like? What were you doing? Who was involved? Where were you living? What was memorable about the experience, and why?

- What makes you smile from within?

- When are you at your happiest? Who is involved? What are you doing?

Chasing the Passion requires focus, drive and persistency. I have learned that you have to pursue and press forward even when you are not up for it! Uncovering the passion in my life and ultimately my purpose has opened doors I never knew were closed. I have pushed through the pain of failure, divorce, and disappointment. I encourage you to dig within to find your purpose and thus your passion!

4 OVERCOMING CHALLENGES

Face it…Overcoming challenges is NOT easy! If achieving success were easy, everyone would do it quickly and without trials. Challenges are NECESSARY! Challenges help us grow as individuals and they are necessary to improve our skills and talents. Most importantly, challenges help us discover who we truly are and what we can accomplish in difficult situations.

Stephen R. Covey once said, "Opposition is a natural part of life. Just as we develop our physical muscles through overcoming opposition- such as lifting weights-we develop our character muscles by overcoming adversity and challenges."

YOU ARE UP TO THE CHALLENGE! Expecting and planning for difficult times helps you prepare to some degree. Establishing contingency plans that address a strategic approach to sustainability. Such plans include achievable goals, resources, strategic partnerships, and potential funding sources. When you can't do anything else you just stand! I have had those days where all I could do was stand. There have been such rocky moments in my journey BUT I have stayed the course and learned that no matter what- it is all a part of the plan. Embracing the experience enough to note the lessons learned and capturing the experience in the form or journaling was a game changer for me.

"To remain indifferent to the challenges we face is indefensible. If the goal is noble, whether or not it is realized within our lifetime is largely irrelevant. What we must do therefore is to strive and persevere and never give up". - **UNKNOWN**

Success is often the reward for hard word and dedication. Remain vigilant in your pursuit to overcome and press toward the mark! You have goals to accomplish, people to help, ideas to develop and businesses to birth. Finding value in the challenges of life helps develop character. Character is needed to drive forth the passion to live out your true purpose in life. Where some see impenetrable barriers, successful people see challenges as learning experiences to grow from.

You will never get used to overcoming challenges but you can get better at planning and accepting all that comes with the experience.

Here are some of the most common obstacles to success:

Time

Lack of Focus

Lack of Dedication

Attitude

It is extremely important to understand the power of your voice. It means establishing the example from which those behind you can follow and reaching forward to those who have paved the way before you to further understand impact and influence. However difficult the obstacle, we must continue to support exaggerated views and recognize that expectations of tolerance for disparities continue to plague our communities, schools, churches, businesses, and homes.

The skilled and advanced insertion of the necessary voice through the input of those that have experience, wisdom, and knowledge is essential as we seek to overcome obstacles. Increase your impact and influence across those vehicles that help catapult you and those around you to success.

Embrace all that you are so that you can find what truly drives you and thus discovering your passion. We are all called for a purpose. Living out that purpose produces a roller of coaster of emotions. Buckle up, hold on tight and seek to amaze, inspire, educate and influence!

"Success is to be measured not so much by the position that one has reached in life as by the obstacles which he has overcome while trying to succeed." - Booker T. Washington

ABOUT THE AUTHOR

Audra T. Jones hails from Cleveland, Ohio where she serves as an entrepreneur, author, speaker, volunteer, and educator. Audra attended Hampton University receiving her Bachelor of Arts in English Arts. She also holds a Masters of Business Administration from Baldwin Wallace College. Audra serves as founder and CEO of Krystal Klear Communications, L.L.C., a Full Service Creative Design firm that specializes in helping small businesses who are overwhelmed with the details and planning of an event by delivering luxury event design and execution services to help create memorable and one of a kind experiences. Audra is the creative behind this literary collaborative project. She is also the author of *Igniting Personal Passion: Manifesting Dreams* and *The Journey Journal.*

Ms. Jones was nominated for The 2014 Young Business Leader of the Year award and received honors as a recipient of the 2014 Amazing Woman award. Audra has served as the Educational Insights and Teaching Techniques Seminar Director and teaches at several colleges around Northeast Ohio. Ms. Jones was also a 2013 and 2014 Honoree featured in the 9th and 10th Editions of Who's Who in Black Cleveland. She has served on the Speaker's Bureau for Congresswoman Marcia L. Fudge, served as a guest panelist for the Women of Color Foundation, received the 2016 John H. Bustamante Emerging Entrepreneur of the Year Award, served as the 2016 Keynote Speaker for the Claude E. Watson Scholarship Fundraising Banquet and the Mistress of Ceremony for the 1st Annual Boss Awards hosted Cuyahoga Community College.

Krystal Klear Communications, L.L.C.

www.krystalklearexperience.com

216.387.0375 | info@krystalklearexperience.com @krystalklearex

AUDRA T. JONES, M.B.A.

03

CHAPTER

03

PERSEVERE THROUGH THE FEAR

DEBORAH GIPSON MOODY

PERSEVERE THROUGH THE FEAR

PART 1
LOVE AND FEAR

LOVE and FEAR--The two most powerful emotions we possess. I believe they are the two motivating factors for everything we do. Both can make us do things we never thought we would. We probably struggle as much with love as with fear, although few would admit to struggling with either. You can't help who you love, but you can control what you fear.

Why do we struggle so much with these two emotions? I believe it is because they are not easily understood, they are not controllable and they can be concealed in many forms. They were the first emotions created, making them the most powerful. Everything we do and feel is just a version of these two feelings. Sometimes they are intertwined making it extremely difficult to understand why we behave the way we do. I believe these two emotions rob us of peace, happiness, confidence, and a fulfilling life. But I believe that with faith, we can *Persevere Through the Fear.*

"Love is what we were born with. Fear is what we learned here."
~Marianne Williamson

PART 2
MY GREATEST FEAR

My greatest fear was not failing myself, but failing others. I felt like I could live with my own personal failures, but not the responsibility and guilt when others entrusted me with tasks or information and I let them down. I felt it showed little faith and even less integrity.

As a child I was painfully shy. I grew up in the suburbs of Sacramento in an environment where people were curious to know more about me and I was content to know less about them. Being black in a predominantly white environment wasn't always easy; it came with its own set of fears. 'Fitting in' or learning how to 'stand out' for more than just the color of my skin, was a challenge. At the time, I could not see that there would be rewards for those challenges, later in life. I have since learned that anytime you face a challenge it can be viewed as a 'character-building' experience. I confess that it was these special times that shaped me into the woman I have become today. It helped me to be accepting of others regardless of skin color, preconceived ideas or economic status.

In retrospect, I realize that I have lived the greater part of my life in fear. I now know that I am not alone. Many people are living in fear, but it is not always apparent. I have also come to know that others who are living in fear have developed effective ways of masking that fear. Sometimes through silence, others through vices, but with the majority, it is behaviors. Recognizing these behaviors is the key. Realizing what we criticize in others, are traits we also possess.

I don't remember how or where it began, I just know how fear affected my life. If I had been able to conquer it sooner, things would have been different. How are you supposed to change the world and make a difference when you are too afraid to speak up or stand up? It is so much easier to give up! You cannot change the world unless you can change your perception of the world. Changing your perception eventually changes your reality.

The more you fear, the less you succeed. Fewer accomplishments, fewer opportunities to make a difference and before you know it, the devil has you right where he wants you; silenced, bound and paralyzed with fear. Have you ever noticed that when you are trying to do a good thing he has a habit of rearing his ugly head to disrupt your thoughts and actions, change your focus and take you off a task? As long as we are off task and not focused, nothing gets completed. Fear is his weapon of choice and we are easy targets.

I believe that fear, failure and faith are all intertwined. They work together for the good and certainly for the not so good. We fear taking action because we are afraid of failure. Not taking action frees us from any responsibility, accountability or judgment. Fear makes us afraid to try because we are afraid to fail, but faith encourages us to persevere. Surviving challenges builds character as well as confidence. Every time we fail, we are given a choice, wallow in self-pity or learn from the failure and move forward. Advancing forward with faith through the difficulty builds confidence and replaces the fear. So when you face a challenge, acknowledge it, accept it, and take action to persevere through that challenge, regardless of the fear.

The definition of failure is the lack of success, the omission of expected or required action. Meaning, the actions you took did not yield the expected results, IT failed, not YOU. YOU are not a failure. Fear can make you think and act like a failure, until you understand the difference.

Fear and faith have something in common.
They ask us to believe in something we cannot see.

~*Joel Osteen*~

How does faith play into this scenario? God uses our 'failures' as a basis to mature us. Moving forward these failures will be referred to as 'challenges'. 'Failure' has a negative connotation and makes it easy for us to give up while, the word 'challenge' encourages us to push forward. As life presents challenges, our faith becomes stronger, making fear weaker. Fear is a burden that we carry around. Every time we are faced with a challenge our load gets heavier. If we do not lighten the load it can eventually break us down, consume us and bring us to our knees under the weight. When God gives you a trial that brings you to your knees that is exactly where he wants and needs you to be. Where HE is the only one you can turn to. Where you have to trust in him with all YOUR heart; and lean not on your own understanding.

How do *you* respond to fear? Does fear force you to take a stand and be bold or does it send you packing, keeping you from achieving your dreams? But once you turn the burden over to Him, he will carry that load. Life changes. You are empowered by his strength. There is a boldness that replaces the fear. You become confident and victorious.

PART 3
EVERYBODY HAS A STORY

Allow me to share my story of fear, failure, and faith. How fear paralyzed me to the point where I felt I could not and did not want to go on.... But mercy said, No!

I own my own business. If that isn't reason enough to be 'fearful'? I work in the wedding industry. I do training, education and personal development. Sounds simple enough. Simple yes, but not always easy.

I acquired the company from the founder, who was a dear friend and mentor. It was 18 years old at the time. As with a child, 18 years is when you let go and send your baby off into the cold, cruel world. So I felt an overwhelming sense of responsibility. Failure was not an option. The opportunity was a blessing and I was grateful. So the journey began.

I was working to modernize the program, when I decided to produce a conference that would enhance education and invite much needed publicity. If you have ever produced a conference you know there is an enormous amount of time and work required to make it successful.

We progressed with promises of funding and helpers. As we all know, life happens! Things changed. But we proceeded because it was necessary for the growth of the company, and unknowingly, for me personally.

We had a great line up of well-known industry speakers, great workshops, a wonderful networking event and the gala banquet. All systems were ago, until they weren't. Funding changed, helpers faded, and attendance was at a less than optimal level. Needless to say the financial burden fell on my shoulders since I was the "fearless leader". But was I? Leader? Yes. Fearless? No. Although initially it seems so, that was not the case. As the date grew closer, anxiety began to build. (Stress and anxiety; stepping stones on the road to fear.)

I was consumed with surviving. I frequently heard statements like, "It will all work out.", "Oh poor thing she seem a little stressed." A little stressed, they had no idea. I had no idea. I was on the edge of a full, complete and utter break down. Trying to work, trying to run a business, to fulfill other life commitments, it all became too much. Fear that this event could be a 'failure' began to take hold. Trying to move forward with that fear became more of a challenge and a greater burden each day. Suddenly or maybe it wasn't so sudden, but because I was so wrapped up in trying to survive, I did not notice, my life was changing. I was forging my way through each day trying to use any distraction I could think of to keep my mind off of the situation. I felt distracted, detached and defeated. Depression engulfed me. Who wouldn't be depressed? I soon found solace in sleep, where I did not have to think, if I could clear my mind long enough to fall asleep. I had little interest in conversing because it required thinking. I was so tired of thinking and trying to figure it all out. I wanted to give up.

My husband did not recognize the stranger he was living with. Heaven forbid he should say anything 'wrong' that would send me into a tirade over some small insignificant thing. My mother and sister were afraid to talk to me for fear of me completely cracking. I was truly wavering on the edge of sanity. I needed a lifeline, which I could not get from my husband, mother, sister, friends or the saints. I could not even attend church for fear of breaking down and flooding the sanctuary. I remember my pastor asking me if I was alright one morning, as we entered the sanctuary. All I could do was shake my head, saying, yes. What could he do at this point? Stop to talk to me when there was a sanctuary full of people, with "real problems" waiting to get a word of encouragement, a prayer of hope.

All the reassurances man tried to offer me were viewed as sincere, but empty promises. I had my prayer warriors on the job, but it was just not enough! They could not help me and I could not help myself. Their prayers could only pacify, not rectify the situation or justify what I was feeling.

I recall the last day of suffering, vividly. I remember waking up, although I did not want to. I wanted to pull up the covers and stay in a mindless sleep zone forever. I got up, I dragged myself into my office, I planned to sit in my chair, but I found myself on the floor, on my knees praying to God. Crying out, "Help me, Lord. I cannot do this any longer. Help me, please! I cannot go on." I begged him to take this burden or take me. I did not care which, at the time, I just knew I was finished and could not go on without help, without him. This may sound dramatic, but I assure you, what I felt was real.

Suddenly nothing changed, but everything changed. It is hard to explain what happened, but I was no longer worried about the outcome. I came to the realization that, it would be what it would be! The 'yoke of fear' and that heavy burden had been lifted. I could actually breathe again. I felt 100 pounds lighter.

I realized that I had to stop trying to control it and let God, be God. I had to accept that I had no real control over anything and yet I still tried to control everything. He is the one who is in control of every situation, not ME, not YOU. Once I figured that out, everything changed. I could move forward. I focused on making it the best event it could be whether there were 18 or 80 people.

You've heard the expression, "Eighteen to eighty...blind, cripple or crazy." How appropriate. I was blind to the fact that God would help me through this situation. I was crippled with fear. And I was crazy with grief and anxiety. I tell my friends that this experience took years off my life, but that it also made me stronger, wiser, and bolder. I became empowered by faith and I *persevered through the fear.* Now when someone asked about any fearful situation, I jokingly say, "that doesn't scare me, I survived the conference." I can now laugh about it. More importantly I can use this experience to help others.

We had the conference. It was excellent, except for the lower than expected turnout. God showed me his favor and mercy and let me know that everything was going to be alright, when unknowingly, the first speaker ended his presentation with one of my favorite poems, *Our Deepest Fear.*

Grace Roberts

"Our Deepest Fear"

Our deepest fear is not that we are inadequate.

Our deepest fear is that we are powerful beyond measure.

It is our light, not our darkness

That most frightens us.

We ask ourselves

Who am I to be brilliant, gorgeous, talented, fabulous?

Actually, who are you not to be?

You are a child of God.

Your playing small

Does not serve the world.

There's nothing enlightened about shrinking

So that other people won't feel insecure around you.

We are all meant to shine,

As children do.

We were born to make manifest

The glory of God that is within us.

It's not just in some of us;

It's in everyone.

And as we let our own light shine,

We unconsciously give other people permission to do the same.

As we're liberated from our own fear,

Our presence automatically liberates others.

~Marianne Williamson

This poem reaffirmed that He was in the midst and that it would be alright. The important thing is that I learned some valuable lessons. These life lessons have been the catalysts for me to use my story, and my testimony to help others. I have been changed by this experience. I feel the journey is just beginning.

Now that the foundation has been set, I would like to share with you some insights about fear. I don't want anyone to go through what I went through. Sharing a few examples, tools and helpful habits might benefit you in overcoming some of your fears or at the very least, view fear differently.

When did we develop such a close relationship with fear? I am not sure but, remember you were taught to be fearful, now you will have to be trained to be fearless!

I had the opportunity to speak at a Christian conference on the subject of 'Fear'. My session was at 8:00 am on a Saturday morning. I was amazed to be received by over 120 women. How could so many people be afraid? What were they afraid of? What could I tell them that would make it all better? Why would so many Christian women be afraid when, "Be not afraid" is the most repeated commandment in the Bible. God did not give us a spirit of fear, but of power, and a sound mind. So why do we struggle so much with fear?

They were looking to me to give them some answers. As I began to share my thoughts, I realized I was completely unafraid. I was excited about the possibility of helping. They needed to know and I was happy to share my experience and give them some insights. I wanted them to recognize the feelings, but more importantly, I wanted to give them ideas on how they could eliminate those fears. After all, what good is knowing, when you don't have tools to fix it.

PART 4
FEAR FACTORS

L et's first examine some of the most common fears that hold us back. You may be surprised when you really analyze it and understand where the emotion resides. Most of our common fears are based on nothing more than judgment; other people's perception of us. We are not really afraid of public speaking, failing or succeeding, the unknown or taking risks. We are afraid of the judgment that surrounds these actions.

Areas of Fear: Judgment, Control, Responsibility, the Unknown and Accountability

Fear of Public Speaking

Are you really afraid of public speaking? It should actually be referred to as public presentation. You speak in public all the time; at the mall, in a restaurant, at work. What is the difference? It is not public speaking you are afraid of but, "public judgment!" What if I say the wrong thing? What will people think? Public speaking requires you to be accountable for what you're presenting. You are perceived as the expert in that area, which requires you to be responsible. Responsibility brings on judgment. Nobody likes to be judged. So what you are really afraid of is the **judgment.**

Fear of the Failure

Are you afraid to fail? You can't fail, if you don't try. We think we are afraid to fail because we think that people will judge us based on our failures. 'We' are never failures 'the event' was unsuccessful, not us. There was simply a miscalculation in the planning process. As a planner, I know that you can plan to the last detail and even have a back-up plan, but this does not ensure the outcome. There are markers for every aspect, but some things are out of our control. We make decisions based on the information that we have at the time and we do our best with the information we are given. We weigh the options, make our choices and wait for the outcomes. What we fear is not failure, but the lack of **control** over the situation.

"What great thing would you attempt if you knew you could not fail?"
~Robert H. Schuller ~

Fear of the Success

How could anyone be afraid of succeeding? You had an idea, you pursued it, and you achieved it. You are a success! Now what? With success comes responsibility. We don't always want to be responsible, because it requires us to be in charge of the outcome, good or bad. It requires that we be held accountable for our actions and responsible for the end results. "Where much is given, much is required." As Christians even more is expected. "There is a burden in the blessing." (T.D. Jakes). Remember, God doesn't call those who are equipped. He equips those who are called. What we fear is not success but, **responsibility.**

"Success is often achieved by those who don't know that failure is inevitable."
~ Coco Chanel ~

Fear of the unknown.

Fear of the unknown prevents us from taking risks. Any successful business person will tell you that at one time or another they took a risk to get where they are now. Fear of the unknown hinders us from asking for that raise or higher position, from really seeking out what we desire. It prevents us from leaving an undesirable situation rather than risk venturing into the unknown. Until the pain of staying, outweighs the pain of leaving, we won't make that change.

We stay in unhappy marriages, unfulfilling relationships, unexciting jobs and other unpleasant environments. We are stuck, not just physically, but also mentally and emotionally. We dare not dream of the possibilities of what might be. Women, in particular are afraid of trusting our instincts and following our gut, maybe because we followed our heart at one time and it did not turn out the way we expected. But what if it turns out better than what we could imagine?

Some people are even afraid to dream, to envision another life. We are happy to simply exist, instead of living. We don't want to disappoint or be disappointed. We think it may not come true. We will never know if we don't take chances. We even impose these thoughts on our children when we tell them to "stop daydreaming and get back to work." Now they are afraid to dream. We should encourage them to dream and to write the dreams down. Then tell them they can achieve any dream through hard work.

Don't let the 'What ifs' deter you. What if I don't? What if you do? What if I lose? What if you win? What if I fail? What if you succeed?

Ignore the fear and focus on the victory! What we fear is not the unknown, but we fear taking a **risk.**

Fear of Judgment

Our most common fear is judgment. This is the one fear that links all the others fears together. We worry about rejection and acceptance. We are constantly being judged and judging others. No one can determine our fate but God, yet we place importance on what everyone else thinks. So does judgment from others really make a difference? It is not really the judgment that worries us, but the accountability. We are afraid to assume accountability over our lives.

It becomes so easy for our judgment to become impaired. "If you don't stand for something, you will fall for anything." As women we need to stand firm in our beliefs and in ourselves. Even in the market place, we receive less pay for the same job. What will they think if I ask for a raise? Who cares what they think? When *they* are paying your bills, then *they* can have an opinion.

So often, perception is not reality and other people's perception of us is just a one-sided picture of what they believe to be true; their view, their opinion and their conclusion. We need to be more accountable to ourselves and stop fearing what others might perceive. The truth is, that it is easier to let them think what they want, that way, we feel we will not be held accountable. Accepting accountability for our actions, even when we think no one is watching, shows integrity. This means there is a standard to maintain. Can you maintain the standard of accountability? Judge not, that you be not judged. Fear of judgment is really, the fear of **accountability.**

It seems as though all the things we think we are afraid of are really just sub categories of judgment, so if we rid ourselves of the fear of the judgment most of our problems surrounding fear, could be resolved. There is an expectation. Can we live up to it? We judge ourselves. We fear we cannot.

We should only be fearful when being judged by God. His judgment is the only judgment that really matters. We should learn to live a life of authenticity on purpose, not judgment.

PART 5
FEAR MANAGEMENT

How do we overcome or manage our fears? Faith, changes the way we view fear. If we were more faithful, we would be less fearful. But first we need to understand the source of fear, then we can look at it differently. We can change the way we look at fear by, changing our language, breaking old habits and developing new practices. Reassessing fear can empower us to be courageous.

Courage is not the absence of fear, but having enough faith to feel the fear, and do it anyway; to *persevere through the fear*. But what if we could remove the fear?

Instead of fear being referred to as: **F**alse **E**vidence **A**ppearing **R**eal

We could replace with: **F**reedom **E**merging **A**fter **R**eality.

Once you locate the real source of the fear, *YOU REALIZE THE FEAR IS NOT AS IT SEEMS, FREEDOM EMERGES AND* the situation no longer hinders you. We can **e**merge with focus, faith and **f**reedom!

Consider the following points.

Procrastination

Procrastination is a symptom of fear, although few view it as such. We look at it like a bad habit, which it is. We put things off because we are afraid to deal with them, afraid it will take too much time or afraid of the outcome. Nike says, "Just do it!" First thing, if possible, so that it does not ruin your whole day by putting it off.

"Learn to defeat procrastination by paying less attention to your fears and more attention to your responsibilities."

Self-induced anxiety

Remove "self-induced" fear. Example: When calling a creditor or a client. Sometimes we talk ourselves into thinking that the situation is much more difficult than it really is, when it could probably be solved with clear communication in many cases. Instead we should take action and do it with diligence, urgency and focus.

Recognition

Acknowledge the fear and determine why it frightens you. Find out what's holding you back, deal with it and move on! When you are able to locate the source of it, you can capture it, contain it and destroy it! Take into account, Fear is often masked by anger, guilt, disappointment and pain.

Victimization

Stop playing the victim. "Half the people don't care what happened, the other half are happy it happened to you, not them." (Les Brown) Don't be victimized by fear. Remember in self-defense courses the first thing you are taught is that attackers look for those who they think cannot defend themselves. "Don't behave like a victim."

Attitude

Stop reacting to fear and change your attitude toward it, you ALWAYS have a choice. It is not what happens, but how we react to what happens. Be courageous and confident. You are the boss of YOU! Be guided by faith, not fear.

Fueled by Passion

When stepping out on faith there is little room for fear or failure. Your faith will allow room for love, acceptance and passion. When times become challenging, you will need love and passion to drive you forward. Priscilla Shirer says, "Passion is the fuel in the engine of purpose. It is what keeps you moving in the direction your best intentions want you to go." Fear drains our fuel and set up a road block for possibilities.

When we love what we do and are passionate about it,
When we know who we are and understand whose we are,
When we accept his will and follow his instruction,
Our passion will guide us, no fear can stop us!

Words can hurt you!

Change your language:

Replace the word 'fear' with; fearless, faithful, courageous and powerful.

Replace the term: "I was afraid." to, "I was concerned, worried or anxious."

This language deescalates fear. Fear starts off small and escalates into panic, fright, and depression.

Synonyms for fear: worry, stress, anxiety, restlessness, uncertainty, concern, apprehension, scared, dismay, dread, trepidation, foreboding, and insecurity.

Recognize these emotions. If you are feeling any of these emotions, you are experiencing a form of fear.

Cover-ups and Lies

Don't let fear draw you into a pack of lies. Think back to childhood when you did something bad. You feared that someone would find out, so you lied to cover it up. Then you were afraid someone would find out that you lied. When they found out, you feared punishment for the action and the lie. As a child you feared the punishment, as an adult you fear the judgment. You feel guilty. Guilt is a by-product of fear. Wouldn't it be easier to just confess your mistakes, and ask for forgiveness?

Prayer Changes Things

We know prayer changes things, but few know how to pray without ceasing? Pray, pray and pray again, be specific and intentional. When you can no longer pray, call your intercessors and warriors. It is not enough to just pray, you have to have a desire for change. You can't receive God's promises if you are afraid to believe that you will.

Talk it out with your true girlfriends. You may be surprised how someone else can enlighten you and put things into perspective. Remember there is always someone worst off than you. Get a new perspective!

Behavior

Change your behavior. Stop stressing over things you cannot change. Fear is simply stress on steroids. Reduce the stress, remove the fear. Fear is sometimes masked as anger because it is easier to show anger than fear. Anger is hard, tough. Fear shows vulnerability. Vulnerability is seen as a weakness instead of a reality of life. It should really be viewed as an opportunity to receive help or help someone else.

Overwhelm

Definition of overwhelm is 'an excessive of anything'. We become overwhelmed when we are over committed. We fear we cannot complete all that is required in the time frame given. Ladies, it is ok to "Just say, No!" You do not have to fear not being liked because you said, No. Better to say no in the beginning than to have to de-commit later. People will respect you more when you acknowledge your limitations. It will still get done. It may even give someone else a chance to show their gifts and be recognized.

Authenticity

Authenticity is the ultimate truth. The truth will set you free and bring you peace. When someone is transparent with you there is a level of trust and a bond that develops. Not being authentic is not living up to your full potential, or being truly free. Freedom is empowering. So be truthful, honest and authentic. Be transparent.

Healthy living

Fear is the number #1 killer of dreams, hopes and possibilities. It takes away a life of peace, fulfillment and happiness.

Fear poisons our systems, causing them to be toxic. Are you filled with jealousy, envy, guilt and unforgiveness?

- Fear is like a cancer; it invades your body and eats away, soon taking over. Don't let it overtake you.

- Stress causes high blood pressure, headaches, chest pains and a rapid heartbeat. Learn to manage your stress.

- Heart disease keeps your heart from functioning properly. The heart is the lifeline to all parts of the body. When the heart is not functioning properly it prevents us from loving; ourselves and others. Don't be afraid to follow your heart!

Journaling

As young girls we used to keep a diary. It was a way of expressing our thoughts and feelings. That remains true. Writing down our thoughts is therapeutic. It allows us to express what we are feeling without judgment. Going back and reviewing where we were at that season of our lives shows how far we have come. Journaling helps us see how much our feelings have changed, how much we have matured, and if we have fulfilled our dreams.

Conquer Fear with Confidence

Confidence is infectious. Instead of infecting people with negative attitude, how about infecting them with confidence, with a boldness that helps them know they can accomplish anything they desire or God's desires for them. Bishop Dale Bronner says, "Stop feeding your insecurities. Whatever you feed grows."

As I described these behaviors it will be easy to say, "I know someone who acts like that." Keep in mind, that someone you know may just be YOU! It is easy to recognize these behaviors in someone else, but we are less likely to acknowledge them in ourselves. Take a moment to self-reflect.

PART 6
PEARLS OF WISDOM

Goal Setting

Fear will keep us from making plans for the future. I believe planning is the key to any successful event, including life, since life is an event. It is important to have a plan for your life. Your plans may change; in fact, you should expect your plans to change as your life changes.

It is important to remember to write down your plans and goals. A goal is just a thought until it is written down. This is separate and different from a journal or diary. Goal setting is a good way of tracking your plans. Write down your goals and then devise a plan on how to achieve them. This is necessary to keep you on track. Goals have to be S.M.A.R.T. Specific, measurable, attainable/achievable, realistic, and timely. *"Write the vision And make it plain. That he may run who reads it."*

Know Your Position

Stay in your lane. Everyone is not designed to be a leader. Some are designed to lead and some are designed to follow. Not all people can be or should be number one. Every good leader needs an even better number 2. It is better to be a great number 2 than to be a bad number 1. Fine your position and be the best you can be, in your role. "Too many chiefs and not enough Indians" make for chaos and impedes progress. Don't be afraid to hold your position or to step up when called to a new role.

Support System

A good leader needs a good support system. Do you ever wonder why some things don't work when *you* did everything right? Maybe *you* were not supposed to do everything. Did you have the support you needed? Were you afraid to ask for help? As women, we do not like to ask for help. It is seen as a sign of weakness. When in fact it should acknowledge that we understand our limitations and we are willing to work with what we have or request what we need. Which is more important, pride or productivity? Surround yourself with the right people to ensure success.

Note: Don't be afraid to persevere when you don't receive the support from the people you expect to endorse or recommend you. Sometimes you have to encourage yourself.

Don't Block Your Blessings

By nature we are givers, nurturer and servants, so our needs often go unfilled. We have servant's hearts, but even servants have to be served on occasion! It is good to receive a blessing. It is humbling and it gives us a chance to show our gratitude. Don't worry. Everyone who blesses you is not looking for something from you in return. The great thing about blessings is that both people are blessed, not just the receiver. Don't block your blessings.

Do It With Love

Mavis Staples father, gave her good advice when she was starting her singing career. He told her to sing from the heart. In all you do, do it from the heart. If it is done from the heart, it will be done with love. Anything accomplished from love is done with passion, focus and clarity and without fear. If you do it from the heart it will be pure, honest and authentic. It will be a blessing and you will be blessed in return.

You are Valuable and Worthy

We spend our lives helping others, but take little time for ourselves. We pour out and we pour into others constantly. Is it because we are afraid to help ourselves or be alone with our thoughts? Sometimes we are busy being busy; running from ourselves. We are afraid to recognize what is missing in our lives. Our inadequacies, shortcomings, our needs and desires.

It is time to recognize our value and worth and use our gifts. In business, one of the biggest hindrances (fears) is not knowing how to charge for our products or services. I believe that is because we do not understand how much the service is worth or how much value we as individuals, bring to that service.

If you are not a business owner, think about how much your presence is worth and how much value you bring to someone else's life, just by being you; being a real friend and being unafraid to be honest. It is acceptable to recognize your value as a person. You don't have to 'do' anything, but be who you already are. You are worthy!

Fear - Your Neighbor

TD Jakes says that Fear and Faith are neighbors. They cannot occupy the same space, but they can live near each other. Imagine you and your neighbor's yard. If there is no fence, no boundary, what keeps something out of your yard? Fear can creep over into your yard and take over. You have to show a clear boundary of your faith. Surround yourself with the word of God and protect your peace and joy. Otherwise fear will creep over and start moving closer to your door. Let fear pass over you and your household. Fear! You are not welcome here!

Favor in the Fear

God brought you through, that was the favor. You thought he wouldn't, that was fear. You doubted God and created your own suffering. The real lesson was that your faith grew stronger, your fear became weaker. You learned that you can't control it all and that prayer was the key. You learned that you had to get out of the middle so God could work and the sooner you did, the sooner it was resolved. God gave you favor even though you were afraid to trust him. He gave you a testimony. There can't be a testimony without a test. You can't have favor without faith. There was favor in your fear.

Ebbs and Flows

Life has ebbs and flows. Don't be afraid to ebb with the challenge and flow towards the victory. Success comes from riding the tide and persevering through the storm. Many people got to be great by being students of life, not afraid to learn from others or to ask for help. Don't be afraid to admit you don't know it all and to accept counsel from someone wiser? If you could see yourself the way God sees you, you would never be fearful. You would be faithful, courageous and victorious!

PART 7
I HAVE LEARNED

We spend a lot of time trying to figure out who we are, when we should be trying to find out why we are, they way we are. Why we are special, why we need to use our uniqueness to our advantage. Why so much time is spent on copying others, instead of creating for ourselves. While it is much easier to copy what someone else is doing rather than reinvent the wheel, remember a copy is never as sharp as the original. That is why God made us all different. We spend too much energy trying to fit in, when we should be trying to stand out.

It is exhausting trying to live up to the standards other people have set for us. We don't have to 'keep up appearances'. It becomes a choice and a privilege to be who God created us to be. We were all designed to be different, giving us our unique personalities, gifts and talents. The problem occurs when we try to take someone else's skills and use them for our purposes. Most people do not even know all of their special gifts because they have not taken time to explore them. We are so busy looking outside that we forget to look inside. Don't be afraid to look inside, you may like what you see. If you don't, you have the option to change.

We are afraid to be ourselves because we are afraid we will not be accepted. Again with the judgment and the perception. Perhaps if we learn to love ourselves, the good, the bad and the ugly we would be much happier. Nobody likes a fake! We are much more intrigued by people that are real, genuine and authentic.

75

We love to dream. Our dreams are where our passions lay. Passion and love keep us motivated when we become fearful and our dreams seem impossible to achieve. Never let anyone or anything, including fear, steal your dreams. If they steal your dreams, they steal your passion, if they steal your passion, they steal your love. And what is life without love? You never know where your dreams might take you. Many dreams have been stolen by fear. You have to persevere.

PART 8
"CLIMB 'TIL YOUR DREAM COMES TRUE"

Climb 'Til Your Dream Comes True

Often your tasks will be many,
And more than you think you can do.
Often the road will be rugged
And the hills insurmountable, too.

But always remember, the hills ahead
Are never as steep as they seem,
And with Faith in your heart start upward
And climb 'Til you reach your dream.

For nothing in life that is worthy
Is never too hard to achieve
If you have the courage to try it
And you have the Faith to believe.

For Faith is a force that is greater
Than knowledge or power or skill
And many defeats turn to triumph
If you trust in God's wisdom and will.

Helen Steiner Rice

PART 9
CONCLUSION

I hope this story will help you to identify what is making you afraid. Whatever that may be, I encourage you to handle it and proceed forward. Once this occurs you can live fuller, richer, more peaceful lives. A life filled with joy courage, passion, freedom, fulfillment and victory!

Fear is binding, but freedom is limitless.

Fear is temporary, but faith is everlasting.

Fear is uncertain, but God is omnipresent.

To everything there is a purpose. We may not always understand it, but maybe we're not supposed to understand it, nor question it. We are however, required to abide, trust and obey.

Every time we are faced with a challenge it is God's way of growing us, preparing us for a higher purpose. Every time we are fearful we doubt God's word and his ability. We are being unfaithful. We know better, especially as Christian women. We know prayer changes things. We know faith conquers fear and we know God's favor is on our lives. So let's stop being afraid to believe and start living on purpose.

There will still be things that make us afraid, but turn that fear over to God. When you do, remember to praise him for his faithfulness, the fear, and the favor that brought you through. Be thankful for the challenges and the blessings. Be grateful for the opportunity to share your story and inspire others.

Praise him for the victory that will be yours, when the fear becomes his!

Persevere Through the Fear!

ABOUT THE AUTHOR

Deborah Moody, Certified Wedding Consultant and Executive Director of Association of Certified Professional Wedding Consultants began her wedding planning career in 1995 and took over as director of ACPWC in 2009. Deborah has represented the ACPWC in Las Vegas, Ireland, China, Maui and Cancun. Deborah attended San Jose University where she studied business. She has been acknowledged in the Cambridge *Who's Who* for leadership and achievement in her profession.

Deborah has been quoted in Black Enterprise, Merrill Lynch Wealth Management Perspective Newsletter, and the San Francisco Chronicle. She had written articles for numerous wedding publications and was featured in Women of Wealth magazine and "Legacies", A guide for Young Black Women in Planning Their Future. Deborah has been a presenter at the BASS (Bay Area Sunday School) and BOTE (Business on the Edge), 'Bridging the Gap Between Business and Faith' conferences and a guest on KDOW radio show.

Deborah was born in Ohio and raised in Northern CA. She is married and currently resides in San Jose, CA. She attends Maranatha Christian Center where she is an active member of the Women of Faith Team and Hospitality Ministries.

DEBORAH GIPSON MOODY

04

CHAPTER

04

RUMBLE YOUNG GIRL, RUMBLE

L.A. HARSH

Rumble, Young Girl Rumble

Who's That Girl?

I have always been that girl who puts too much cream in her coffee. I encounter this life as a gift bearer. Like cream, my presence has been known to enhance the texture of others; adding thickness to the overall experience; changing the taste of life with every sip; masking the traces of bitterness through gulps of smoothness; overpowered by savory sweetness within every cup. If you haven't noticed already I am a poet, a scribe, a wordsmith, a griot of this era, a lover of language and a mistress of the written word.

To begin, I am so much more than a pretty face. I am God's presence—constructed from the Creator's design. I am inspiration. I am the voice within that never dies. I am the subconscious awareness. I am my mother's pride and my father's forgotten treasure. I am perseverance in its darkest hour. I am a healer from a forgotten place; the smile on my children's faces…the mother of the village.

I am a good night's kiss. I am beautiful eyes and smoldering hips. I am unconquerable land. I am deep sleep. I am that light at the end of the tunnel. I am that second look, that deep desire, that constant pleasure. I am an erotic scent— the inscription of beauty. I am faith. Often times, the biggest regret of past lovers. I am an immense love story…the definition of loyalty.

I am heat and fire glowing. I am that fifth element. I am bright shades of yellow. I have a fierce magnetic pull. I am the heart of home. The energy that keeps the cosmos suspended in space. I am pulse. I am height in its full stance. I am friend, never foe…my sisters' and brethren's keeper. I am an honored member of Sigma Gamma Rho Sorority, Incorporated; Gamma Epsilon made on the campus of Kent State University.

I am the opposite of doubt. I am warrior. I will stand and fight. I speak out even when my voice trembles. I am protector—rest safely in my prayers. I am courage—hear me roar. I am hate's opposition. I am daily blessings and solemn prayers. I am forgiveness. I am laughter; again, so much more than just an attractive surface. Simply put...I am a child of God with the tune of *this little light of mine, I'm gonna let it shine* echoing through my soul. Truthfully speaking, it would take decades before I would recognize the depth of my own worth or before I could see the queen within me.

As a child, my roots were planted in a single parent household. When I say single, I mean singular in every sense of the word. There were no stable paternal figures, no elders in the form of grandparents, uncles, or aunts. My mother was the only provider my sister and I truly knew.

Although my mother was often vacant in our lives, working multiple jobs and infinite hours to keep a roof over our heads in the suburbs of Warrensville Heights, Ohio; she was the only constant in our lives and her melodic rhythm expressed a kind, yet, melancholy blues. As a young biracial girl, I often times felt disconnected from the woman I called momma. Through my juvenile eyes, momma and I did not share any commonalities that would make one feel like part of the same ancestry such as last names, hair textures, features, or known form of family legacy.

See momma was a White woman from the southern state of Missouri. I'd later discover, she was renounced by her father

85

and shunned by many in her family for having "Black babies". I still recall with clarity the day I realized my mother was White and I was Black. At four-years-old, I was watching a local news station when I mumbled out loud, "Momma that news lady looks just like you, but she's White."

Momma responded with a chuckle, "But I am White, Fatty (my childhood nickname). You didn't know yo' momma was White?"

To a displaced child growing up in the 70's that phenomenon just didn't make any sense to me. *How could she be White, and we—her offspring—be Black?* Something no one bothered to explain to me as I struggled alone to find my sense of self in a racially divided world. The memories still echo feelings of hatred deeply harbored towards a woman whose only true crime was loving her children. My ignorance and confusion, coupled with a persistent feeling of not "belonging" led to resentment, isolation and disdain. Not at the world or society, as one may expect, but towards my mother.

Unannounced to my youthful awareness, a thing known as interracial marriage would not be legalized until 1967 and it would take the Supreme Court to mandate that right in many states. This historical taboo would only precede my birth by five years and the residue of such race-based restrictions were regularly experienced throughout my adolescence.

My youthful memories were ones met with disesteem, dirty looks, and whispers. Since conception, I laid resting in my mother's womb growing in shame. I came to this earth fighting for my mother's attention and a father's love. As a consequence, I blamed momma for every unkind experience I endured from the humiliation of having to wear my hair in an afro—something I believed at the time to be an unacceptable hairstyle for a young girl, to being mistaken as a boy throughout my elementary years, to the relentless taunting and teasing that the outsiders of a society repeatedly brave.

It's where, as a youth, I would learn to be seen and not heard. End result, many adults labeled me a well-mannered child, but I was honestly just trying to go unnoticed. I didn't want to be questioned about my ethnicity or where my father was or whether or not my mother was the White woman standing at that door to pick someone up. It's ironic how we despise the ones that stay, and idolize those that abandon us.

I now know that it was just easier to blame momma for everything because she was so meek and kindhearted—she would calmly "take one for the team" with no complaints. It was during that time that I mistook kindness as weakness. Momma and I would be unabated polar opposites until the day I finally became a mother and had my own children. It would take the parent-child bond, ignited by my eldest born, to truly teach me how to open my heart to love, respect and admiration for my own mother and eventually myself.

Until that point our mother-daughter relationship would be contentious at best. I intentionally went out of my way to be unlike my mother. Moreover, I had decided early on that I was NOT biracial. I would represent myself as a light skin Black person. I would relax my hair even though it was not needed, I would embrace my African ethnicity while ignoring my other nationalities, I majored in Pan African Studies as an undergraduate, gave my children African names and only acknowledged pride in being of African descent, and yet I had never laid eyes on my biological father or any members of his family.

Sadly, I had become accustomed to playing the victim in my life. My childhood was one met with extreme hardships. Adversities endured would later serve as my greatest teachers in parenting. As I matured, parts of me would learn to appreciate such lessons that stemmed from a neglected childhood. I discovered early on when you don't protect precious things, they get stripped from your possession like a petal from a wild flower.

As life would have it, I would unwillingly lose my innocence at the ripe age of four or five. The aftermath of that ordeal would forever change my disposition regarding "the natural order" of things according to the *universal law of nature*. It would become the primary source of why I grew in such hatred towards my mother during those crucial developmental years. The more I matured in age, the more I grew to despise her— my mother. Because of course from my naive perspective, EVERYTHING was momma's fault, especially being molested at such a young age.

It was at that point in life that I started calling my mother "Toots" just like all the other street kids on our block. I reasoned that she was not worthy of being called my momma. All I could think during those years was, *Who allows their daughter to get abused in such a way? Who leaves their daughters unprotected to be food for the prey.* It would take many years before I was able to unlearn such a victimized mentality.

Those early years would be responsible for producing the victim within me. It is through that trauma that I would endure life as a casualty. I was so angry and withdrawn. I had constructed a wall of protection around me. Throughout high school and possibly college, I was viewed as the "stuck-up girl". I did not ask nor did I seek the attention to be popular, but I found myself in that role nonetheless. I would mask my identity behind name brand clothes, up-to-date trends, and too grown styles. Oblivious to others, I was merely a wounded soul in need of a place to unload concealed feelings of mistrust, betrayal and hurt. As the only adult present, momma was always the perfect target. The smile I once shared with others was unapologetically stripped from my soul for decades. As fate would have it, I had grown into a confused and sometimes difficult teen.

My twenties would prove to be a span of discovery. I embarked upon the campus of Kent State University young, insecure and in search of my sense of purpose. Completely lost unto myself, I was clueless and in need of establishing my identity. Without thought, I would jump from major to major with no direction or certainty as to what I would become in life.

I spent a great deal of my college years, nurtured in the walls of Oscar Ritchie Hall where The Department of Pan African Studies was located. This space always felt like home to my secluded soul. It is where I would discover some of my most beloved poets/writers: Paul Laurence Dunbar's "We Wear the Mask"; Zora Neale Hurston; Jessica Care Moore; Professor (Baba) Mwatabu Okantah; my English 101 teacher, Mrs. Webster; and countless others. It is also where I would find my voice as a poet and a teller of tales.

Opportunely, I have always been a lover of knowledge. Since I can recall, life has been one book after another. If you can imagine, my momma was a hoarder of books. She kept boxes upon boxes of stored novels. She made certain that my sister and me were supplied with an array of literature from various coloring books to magazines to the complete set of Encyclopedia Britannica to every Walt Disney storybook created. As a youngster, I would sit looking through literature or just coloring for hours because there was rarely supervision around when momma was at work and going outside to play was NEVER an option.

Due to momma's work schedule, my sister nor I could go outdoors until momma got home. Often times momma would be gone from sun up to sun down working multiple jobs to clothe, feed, and provide shelter for us. What I lacked in resources, lessons, stories and the wisdom imparted by elders was made up for in books. My village would forever become the literature that surrounded me. It is safe to say that books raised me since my youth filled days.

As previously mentioned, it wouldn't be until much later that I would discover unconditional love with the pregnancy and birth of my first-born, Diallo Niamke. I have always identified him as the anchor that grounded me; leading me off a path of self-hatred and onto a road of self-love. My son has forever symbolized the pillar of strength in my life—my rock. With his birth came balance and resolution to my unsettled presence. His existence spoke vigor to a barren soul. His life charged me with the mission to want more of myself. As a Pan African studies major, my greatest discovery is bested summed up from a James Baldwin quote, "Know from whence you came. If you know whence you came, there are absolutely no limitations to where you can go."

As I began to develop into my womanliness, I started to ask the right questions of myself. The important questions. Those soul-searching questions. Those moments always led me to my safe haven—to a refuge housing the poet within. The artistry of words has always soothed my aching spirit as it offered an expressive outlet.

Beyond the gifts of love between my children and myself, parenting brought many blessings into my life. Motherhood would become the key that opened the door to an intimate relationship with my mother. At 24-years-old, I no longer felt like a motherless child. Momma and I had become long lost spirits reunited. And by the time I had my second child—my lovely Nadia, a constant reminder of promise—momma and I were talking daily. She would call me Monday – Friday around 4:20 p.m. and ask, "So what I miss!?" as we tuned in to the syndicated talk show, 'Oprah", together while chatting or simply holding the phone until our much-loved show was over. Not to mention, I would call her at least once a week while she was at work to inquire about various recipes and seek advice as I cooked dinner for the family. Though I spent so many years trying to be contrary to who I believed my mother to be. I now began to see parts of her within me; and I was glad, strengthened and proud.

Disappointingly that joy would be short lived. Two years after my daughter's birth, I would get the dreaded call from my sister, Janet, announcing our mother was pissed at her and she would probably be contacting me soon to vent. Apparently, my sister called the ambulance and forced our mother to go to the hospital because she wasn't feeling well for some time. Sadly, we didn't foresee recovery any time soon. I'll never forget that call, it was on Hallows' Eve. Our mother would die a month and a half later on December 16, 2003 from stage IV cancer. My life, my heart, my thoughts, my everything forever changed. I discovered an emptiness within that I never knew could exist.

During that time, I happened to be wearing my hair in locks that rested on my shoulders. As I went to visit my mom in the hospital, the dementia that played peek-a-boo with her memory didn't always permit her to recognize me. As young women, my sister and I witnessed our mother toggle between two worlds of reality—the spirit world and this earthly world.

I remember driving home in a daze after visiting my mother in the hospital. I was extremely saddened by this unexpected tragedy especially the sporadic memory loss. It was important to me that in my mother's final days, she knew who I was. I wanted her to see me! I wanted her to recognize her baby girl! I did not want her to leave without saying "goodbye" to her daughter.

As I arrived home that evening, I mechanically placed the key in the lock, opened the door, took my two-year-old daughter's coat off, sat her on the couch, and I proceeded directly to the bathroom. I grabbed a pair of scissors, looked into the mirror, and fighting back the tears, I cut every matted lock from my head. I now had a Florida Evans' afro, just like I did when I was momma's little girl.

The next morning I returned to the hospital. When I entered my mother's room, she was sitting up in the hospital bed. Her face beamed as she yelled, "Fatty!" with her arms stretched opened for a hug. I put my daughter down and ran to my mother's bedside. I placed my chin in the palm of both of her hands as she cupped my face. With those loving hands that once cuddled me as a child, she pulled my face to hers. We touched nose-to-nose as we stared into each other's eyes partially grinning.

Our eyes spoke in silence what words would never reveal. I displayed a genuine smile as I soaked up the warmth from my mother's hands and felt the pulse of her blood. I leaned my head to one side and mouthed to her, "It's ok, momma. Fatty's here. It's ok."

She looked so childlike. And for a moment, I could see another her from a past dimension. I witnessed a pain in her eyes as she responded, "I've been holding on. I've been trying to stay…"

She extended her arm out, reaching for something that I could not see. Then she finished her statement, "…but momma's there. They are all there!" as she jabbed the air with her index finger.

I looked where she was pointing and still saw nothing as she continued to motion with her fingers. She was no longer communicating with me. Her ancestors were present. They had been welcoming her. The vibration in the room was shifting. I could feel my momma pulling away from me. I could feel her longing for her own mother. My eyes opened wide as I took a deep breath and granted my mother approval to slip away from us. I spoke softly as to not offend the living, "It's ok, momma. It's ok to let go. I give you my permission to cross over. I know they are waiting for you. I promise you, we will be ok. I will never let your grandchildren forget you."

As I stared into my mother's elderly brown eyes, it would be the first time I would recognize us in one another beyond sheer similarities. I realized that we actually did share a lot such as that same southern dialect, that same broad nose, that same love for cooking, that same joy for holiday traditions, that same kind heart, that same humble spirit. She was me and I was her. That would be the first time I would consciously let her know I was Judie's daughter. I vowed to be her legacy. I assured her, "We will honor you," as I kissed her forehead as if she was the child and I the mother.

I left that hospital room and instantly called my Aunt Janet, my mother's younger sister. I informed her that my mother would be dying soon and I wasn't sure how much time she had. My aunt and her husband, Uncle Louie, came within days. Their presence allowed me to be a little girl grieving the loss of her mother. It would be the second time I permitted myself to cry since I found out my mother had stage IV cancer. They will never know how needed their presence was to a young girl trying to honor her mother in her last days. I will forever be grateful for them, and the relief their presence afforded during my mother's final days.

Losing my mother has taught me countless lessons. What I have come to learn is that I am my mother's child. Through tremendous loss, I have fully come to accept myself. When I love unto others, my cup overflows with generosity and an undeniable gratitude. It's been said that the people who exhibit the most kindness have experienced the most pain because we live with a constant throbbing that many can't imagine enduring.

Over the years, I have lost many priceless things—the esteem that comes with having a dedicated father, my innocence, my beautiful mother, my marriage, our family home, my concept of family, but the one thing I have NEVER lost is my faith. Through every trail and tribulation, I can still feel the Creator assuring me that it's ok. Reminding me to continue to work through the hurt. Prompting me to keep loving with that big, open heart…even when others disappoint. Encouraging me that under no circumstances do I hold on to the pain…modestly let it all go and learn to let God.

Thus, I have learned to be grateful for each day I experience. I've moved from a victim mentality to victor mindset. I have granted myself the approval to allow my light to shine in hopes that it will stimulate others to do the same in spirit. I truly live by the words of Jeffrey Gitomer, "Resilience is not what happens to you. It's how you react to, respond to, and recover from what happens to you."

I can now accept that I am a giver, a nurturer, a mender of souls and simply put—Judie's daughter. I rarely get jammed up in titles or roles. I've understood my purpose in this world since a very young age. I've come to encourage, to uplift, to speak truth as a woman, a mother, a teacher, and a lover. Constantly reminded by a passage discovered in *Miracles* (1983) that the eternal life force teaches us to advocate, "I am eternal, immortal, universal, and infinite, and what I am is beautiful."

My life, hardships and all, has prepared me to walk in my purpose. I am on the move from a victor mindset to a victorious existence. My journey is nowhere near over. On the contrary, it's just beginning. I can hear God whispering to my spirit, "Get ready to rumble young girl!"

WHERE I'M FROM

I am from homemade cooking, country music, and "chil don't forget yo' manners. From the house of Spades where card games were met by tunes blared throughout all hours of darkness.

I am from southern cooking, overstuffed lasagnas, bread smeared with the sweet taste of butter alongside homespun jams and from single households of maternal ways and forgotten surnames.

I am from the genius of God, the hopes of my momma, the hearts of my children, but I've been knocked down from that place of absentee fathers, distracted partners, and nowhere to be found lovers. From the death of a mother taken too soon to discovering how to let go and let God.

I am from the good book of Proverbs interchanged with the words, "Mommy! I love you to the infinity power!"

I am from the struggles of growing up too fast, lessons learned too slowly, and if I knew then what I know now, I'd be headed to better places.

I am from photos once displayed throughout my momma's house of unruly Afros, Tomboy ways, raggedy tennis shoes and missing front teeth.

I am from a mother's love.

ABOUT THE AUTHOR

L.A. Harsh, is the author *of Lessons Learned: A Woman's Perspective.*

She has also written a collection of poems. She resides in Sagamore Hills, Ohio and is the mother of two inspiring children, Diallo and Nadia Niamke. You can follow her on Instagram @laharsh

L.A. HARSH

05

CHAPTER

05

PATHWAY TO PURPOSE: UNAPOLOGETICALLY ME

JACQUELYN R. JONES, PH.D.

PATHWAY TO PURPOSE:
UNAPOLOGETICALLY ME

My name is Dr. Jacquelyn Renee` Jones and I am a university administrator in higher education administration. I work tirelessly to impact the lives of college students in a meaningful way. I am a first generation college student and one of the first in my family to obtain a terminal degree. I originally hail from Strongsville, Ohio right outside of Cleveland, Ohio, however, I currently reside in Greensboro, North Carolina. Who am I? I am a woman on the move. I am a woman who has passion for greatness; passion for success. I am a family girl, daughter, sister, godmother, cousin, niece, friend, confidant, leader, and the list can go on and on. I have a caring spirit to help others any way I can, be it in my professional or personal life. I am a conqueror in Christ Jesus. I am a child of God who gives him all praises and Glory for my very existence. Throughout my life, I have always been someone that relies on my faith to move me forward in this thing we call life. For as long as I can remember, I have always been driven by success.

Growing up, my mother and father always instilled in my sister and I that we could do or be anything that we put our minds to. Even though my sister and I were first generation college students, attending college was an expectation that my parents had for their girls. After high school graduation, I decided to attend The University of Akron to pursue my bachelor's degree. When my parents dropped me off on campus for new student orientation, I remember being filled with so many emotions. I was excited, nervous, anxious, happy, and sad all at the same time. I was not sure what to expect. During my first moments on campus (before entering orientation session) I met a woman who would later take me under her wing. This woman demonstrated leadership in a way that was admirable, which had a lasting impression on me. She told my mom that day that she would make sure that I was okay and that she would take care of me during my Akron college days.

She has kept her promise. Not only did she make sure that I was connected to resources, but she became my friend, my mentor, my sorority sister and so much more. She may not even realize this, but she was the very reason why I decided to pursue a lifelong career and journey in higher education. She cared so much for her students. We all knew that anything we needed, be it support- academically, emotionally, socially, or mentally, we could go to her office and she was there with open arms ready to assist and serve her students. It is because of this college administrator that I pursued my Master's degree in Higher Education Administration.

It was during my college years where I blossomed into a leader. While on campus, I found myself entrenched in the campus life and connecting with as many people that I could connect with while there. I wanted to make the best of my college experience. I joined clubs and organizations and excelled in my studies. Immediately upon completion of my Bachelor of Science degree, which is in Sport and Exercise Science, I entered graduate school at the same institution. My Master of Science degree is in Higher Education Administration. After graduate school, I relocated to upstate New York to work for a small private liberal arts university. I was in upstate New York for 2 years impacting the lives of college students and working with them on co-curricular education and student activities.

I was living in New York for about 3 months in my first professional job after graduate school and 8 hours away from home. One Monday morning in October, I received a phone call from my mother telling me that my Godmother had passed away. I felt so far away from the reality of her passing. I was very close to her and could not effectively articulate at the moment how I was feeling. I can just remember that going to work that morning was so hard because I missed the presence of my family and was grieving the loss of my Godmother at the same time. Feeling empty throughout that week, I can recall that my family seemed very hurt and troubled as the week progressed; and we were planning for her home going service.

It was decided that her services would be held that upcoming weekend, so quickly, as a family, we decided that I would need to attend her funeral services so I could gain some closure of her passing. Flights were too expensive at that time for my family or myself to afford, so I drove home to Cleveland by myself, which was 8 hours alone. However, I was a soldier and took it like a champ. It was my faith in God, that I knew that even though I had never had to make a trip like this by myself that he would take the wheel for me and ensure my safety. And he did just that. God and I had many conversations throughout that ride and I started to feel at peace. At the same time, my Godfather was also suffering from being sick. I was also very close to him. My first stop would be to drive to my Godfathers house once I made it to Cleveland because I wanted to check on him. However, both my sister and mom kept trying to strategically intercept where I went first and pleaded that I drive to my sister's home first where the entire family would be waiting on my arrival. Finally after I made my mom promise that once I got to my sister's house, we could go and check on my Godfather, I agreed to stopping at my sister's house first. I was greeted with heavy and sad hearts, but happy hearts because we all missed each other. The next moment, my mom sat me down on the couch and delivered the saddest news to me. She informed me that on Thursday of the same week my Godmother passed, my Godfather passed away too. She did not want to deliver the news to me while I was still in New York. He died from a broken heart and missed his wife. She told me that after her passing, he just shut down and stopped eating anything. I was so upset and felt like I was living in the twilight zone. Needless to say, I buried both of my Godparents the same weekend, the same day and there was a double home going service for each one.

While living in New York, it became very lonely because I lived in a small college town, with not much civilization and it dawned on me that this was really the first time in my life that I was this far away from my family. During this time, I had to draw on my relationship with Christ and I was blessed to meet two dynamic women who were also on the same journey in that small town. We became each other's support system as we experienced living in a rural town for the very first time.

It was 2 years later that I was intentional about my next career move. I was offered a position in Maryland with a large, research institution to work with college students and assist with programming on campus. During my transition from New York to Maryland, my grandfather passed away a few days before I was scheduled to have the movers relocate me to Maryland. Dealing with death has always been so hard for me and so here I was again, faced with another loved one's death. At a time in my life where I was supposed to be celebrating a new career move, I was faced with losing my granddaddy who lived in Alabama at the time. Grief is difficult. So as I prepared mentally for his funeral service, all I could do was lean and depend on God and realize that he has brought me over some mountains in my lifetime.

I loved living in Maryland, however the cost of living eventually drove me to the realization that it would be economically more responsible to move to a place where the cost of living was more affordable. The cost of living was so expensive that I found myself having to obtain a second part-time job just to make ends meet.

As I entered into prayer about my next steps, I was told by God to just sit tight and wait for more direction. So I waited. In late winter and early spring, we had some more deaths in our family. This time it was my cousin and one of my uncles. It was these two deaths that made me realize that it was time for me to come back home to Ohio. So I started to pray about my journey again. This time, I heard God tell me to start looking for jobs in Northwest Ohio, which was very interesting because I am from Northeast Ohio. Anytime I contemplate a life change, I always consult with my Heavenly Father because he has not steered me in the wrong direction. God is always there for me because I am blessed and highly favored.

I applied to one job in Ohio and got that job, which would put me just an hour and a half from where my parents and sister lived. It gave me great comfort to know how close I could be to my immediate family. When I first moved back to Ohio, I thought I was passing through for a couple of years, but God had a different plan for my life. I ended up living in Northwest Ohio for nine great years.

Two years after being in the job that relocated me back to Ohio, I was faced with being laid off from my job. Imagine my dismay when I learned that there was a reduction in work force due to budgetary constraints. I was devastated. My emotions ranged from being sad and upset to anger and rage. I could not believe that I was a young woman with a Master's degree and was actually laid off.

At the time of the layoff, I was in my doctoral program for my Ph.D. in Higher Education Administration. As I started to prepare myself for my doctoral studies to become full time, I was approached by the local community college to take a position with them. My career really began to blossom and I was able to work with students who were also first generation college students like myself. I worked with students who were given a second chance and entering college was their greatest accomplishment. I was a part of a department where working with college students was second nature to the team and it was very gratifying to witness the profound impact that my office had on students.

In each of the positions that I have held, God always reminds me of why I was called to higher education. I thank God daily for the gift that he gave me. The students that I worked with faced challenges and barriers that could impact their success and I was blessed with a staff who shared the same gift that I had—impacting the lives of college students, one at a time. During my time in Ohio, I was blessed with many opportunities.

It was in Northwest Ohio where I joined the best sorority on this side of life and earth- Delta Sigma Theta Sorority, Incorporated. I was able to gain 23 beautiful line sisters and so many sorors and friends who I cherish very much because of the sisterhood and bond that comes with being a member of this illustrious sorority. It was in Northwest Ohio where I gained some very valuable friendships and share a strong sisterhood that helped me along my life journey while I was seeking my doctoral degree. I became Dr. Jacquelyn Renee Jones in Northwest Ohio, and while I am so grateful to God that I have this terminal degree, there were a lot of blood, sweat and tears throughout my doctoral journey.

I can remember it so vividly, at the age of 3 years old, running around the house telling everyone in my family that I was going to be a Doctor when I grew up. My mom always called me Dr. Jacquie, instilling this passion and desire to serve others early on in my life. Throughout high school, I thought I wanted to be a medical doctor, but the excitement was not there deep inside. I struggled internally as I thought about what my future would hold, and what my career path would be. All I knew was that being in a field where I could utilize my interpersonal and communication skills would be at the forefront of my decision. I also knew that helping others in ways that they could not help themselves or articulate their needs; would be critical in my career path.

Much to my surprise, my vision and dream of becoming a doctor was clearer and clearer to me after my undergraduate career. I wanted to help others like my mentor did from my alma mater and this is when higher education administration as a career was introduced to me.

Beginning my doctoral journey was so exhilarating and fulfilling. I was a part-time doctoral student and worked full time. I had to be very strategic during my doctoral journey because in my mind, my only option was to be successful in my program. I delved into my coursework, intentional in my classes to soak in all of the knowledge that my professors were teaching me. After all, I wanted to be the best administrator that I could be, apply theory to practice as I was living as a student, transitioning to an academic scholar. As I embarked on the writing phase of my dissertation, I can remember having many sleepless and restless nights. I lived and breathed my research. I was determined to complete my doctoral program within 4 to 5 years of starting. I had a plan. I quickly came to realize during this process that my plan was not always God's plan for my life.

After many drafts, and re-writes of my dissertation chapters, I started to feel hopeless and defeated. The dissertation process for me was a lonely process because no one really knew my struggle. My family and friends tried to support me to the best of their ability, but they could not feel the pain that I was dealing with. My cohort classmates knew the struggle because we were all dealing with similar stories simultaneously, however, I started seeing and witnessing some very distinct differences in my dissertation journey as a African American woman vs. my White counterpart's dissertation journey.

There were many times during my process where I was steered in different directions in what felt like I was being delayed toward completion of my degree. I kept pressing on and praying to my Heavenly Father. I knew that God, the Father, and the Son held my destiny in HIS hands not my committee. My committee had an assignment by God to lead me where I was already destined to get to. They were the vehicles to my success even if sometimes I did not feel supported throughout that process by some, not all. There were many times during the process that I felt like it would never end. I came to the realization that people like to put you through what they went through during their own doctoral process. Nothing could stop me. I was this young, Black woman who is BLESSED and HIGHLY favored and my favor comes from the LORD. No matter how many times my process was stunted, God kept preparing and equipping me to succeed and move forward. God had many people in my dissertation journey who supported my research and spoke for me when I could not speak for myself. I am forever grateful to those individuals (they know who they are) for staying true to me as I transitioned from student, to scholar, to the expert in my study.

I can remember the excitement leading up to my dissertation defense. I can also remember feeling very fatigued from so many changes to my dissertation even at the 11th hour of it being submitted for final approval. The week of my final defense was so draining on me physically, mentally, and emotionally. I remember sitting at my desk and just weeping and crying out to God. I was so sick and tired of being challenged by the results of my study because the results did not come out the way someone may have wanted them to. They kept on wanting me to change things and re-run my data at the 11th hour, that I finally had to stand up to my committee chair and beg for their support while I was dealing with this difficult task. I was supported to continue to the final defense.

I invited my entire support system that included my mom, dad, sister, best friends, prayer partners, colleagues and a few cohort friends. There were 12 people in total that came to my final defense. My chair even mentioned that this was the first time she witnessed that many people at a defense. She knew that this would be a big moment for me. After all, this degree that I was going for was not only for me, but it was for my mom, my dad, my ancestors who paved the way many years ago so that I may have an education, so that I may have opportunities presented to me during my lifetime as a Black woman. I expressed to everyone in the room that they were all part of my village. The African Proverb that it takes a village is so true. The people that came to my dissertation defense were my village of support. They prayed with me, they cried with me, they listened to me and were always there for me throughout my journey to becoming Dr. Jones.

During my presentation, I was literally interrupted by someone on my committee after every single slide – asking me to explain every detail and jumping ahead to what I would eventually get to in following slides. All I could think of was this was the attack of the DEVIL and that no weapon formed against me would ever prosper. The devil was so mad that I was about to be declared Dr. Jones that he tried to put stumbling blocks in my way at my final defense. While hindsight is 20/20, it would have been better if I felt there was a true advocate for me in that moment, however, my advocate was God. It was clear to me that this encounter that I faced was not like any of my other cohort members in their dissertation defenses (because I had witnessed all of their final defenses) and they did not experience any of the same setbacks that I experienced while defending. I stood there in that defense room unapologetic for my success, unapologetically me. I defended my dissertation and I knew I was the EXPERT in my study. In fact, I profoundly realized in that moment that I knew more about my study than anyone in the room because my research was lived and breathed by ME for over a year. I spent countless hours agonizing on what to put in this chapter vs. that chapter. So even while I was standing there and presenting on my topic, I could feel the POWER of the Holy Spirit in that room. God's presence filled that place and I felt his anointing over my life even in that moment. I kept thinking that I was more than a conqueror in Jesus name. I could feel the prayers coming my way from my VILLAGE.

As I completed my presentation, I fielded questions from my committee. During the deliberation, myself and my guests

111

were asked to exit the room so a decision can be made on if I passed or failed. Once we exited the room, my spirit kept saying YES. I prayed that the answer would be YES. Standing outside with my VILLAGE, unapologetic for standing in my destiny, my dad began to pray. My mom and sister began to pray and many others were standing in agreement with me and praying on my behalf while we waited that I would receive favorable news. Once my committee was done deliberating, they asked me to come back in to hear their decision. We all came in one by one. As I entered the room, I felt God's Glory fill up that room when I came back in. His presence was so powerful. His showers of blessings were in that place.

My chair waited patiently for all 12 of us to get completely in the room. She then graciously said, "Dr. Jones congratulations for successfully passing your defense!" The room let out a big loud cheer and all I could do was give God the praise and the glory and the honor for bringing me through that journey and process. I thanked my committee. I hugged my chair and hugged each member in my village! I even recall looking around that room and seeing so many tears of joy for my success. It was one of the few times that I saw my dad cry. They celebrated me, and each person in that room, on that day played a pivotal role in my pathway to success and purpose.

It was that day on Friday, May 10, 2013~ When my committee chair declared me Dr. Jones, my mom started thanking God publicly in front of everyone. She gave it a Holy Ghost SHOUT! Crying to the Lord and thanking him for bringing her baby through that journey. My father cried tears of joy for his baby girl. And my sister kept shouting "Yes Sir" as she was wiping her face from the tears flowing. My friends, family members, prayer partners, cohort friends, and boyfriend at the time also celebrated my news. That was one of the happiest days of my life. I walked the stage at commencement on Sunday, May 12, 2013, where I was hooded by my chair and officially announced Dr. Jacquelyn R. Jones. My family and friends were there to celebrate with me.

Fast forward to a month after my doctoral graduation. I went through a very hurtful and painful breakup with my boyfriend at that time. We dated for a significant amount of time and even talked about marriage. Internalizing some of the obstacles that we faced, which ultimately lead to the breakup, I was not in a good head space during that time. I began to become very angry with him, myself, and God for allowing me and us to go through such hurt and pain. I was reminded in my prayer time that everything in our lives happens for a reason. Even when it was hard and difficult for me to accept losing him as my boyfriend, I knew that our season had expired and it was time for me to move on. I had to seek counseling from a Christian counselor to help work through the pain from the breakup. It was in counseling where I could fully forgive him, myself, and God and become truly healed and delivered from that hurt that I once experienced. I count it a blessing that although it took a few years for us to reconnect as friends again, I am happy to say that he is still someone in my life that I keep in touch with every now and then. It was through Gods love for both of us that he makes it possible for the body of Christ to love each other unconditionally, no matter the circumstances.

It is important to recall that there was a time in my life journey that I struggled with medical challenges. There was so much stress over my life after the breakup and my doctoral degree that my body was reacting to the stress and it manifested in multiple ways. From back pain that was so debilitating and finding it extremely difficult to walk at times, to experiencing a condition in my eye that blurred my vision for two weeks, where it was difficult to see out of one of my eyes. I was scared, frightened, and afraid. And then my mom, who is one of my biggest cheerleaders, instructed me to read scriptures daily that ultimately would change my life. Psalms 23, Psalms 91 and Psalms 100. In addition, she has always embedded in both my sister and I to read Isaiah 40: 29-31 and Ephesians 6: 11-18. I recall during times of dealing with sickness, saying repeatedly to myself that by his stripes I am healed and reading Isaiah 53:4-5~ I started to internalize what "by his stripes" and "we are healed" really meant for me. I knew that my faith needed to be activated so that God could heal me. In my daily devotional time, I thought about "stripes." These stripes were administered by whipping the bare backs of prisoners whose hands and feet were bound, rendering them helpless. The phrase "by His stripes we are healed" refers to the punishment Jesus Christ suffered—whippings and beatings with fists, that were followed by His agonizing death on a cross—to take upon Himself all the sins of all people who believe Jesus Christ is Lord and Savior. "I am the way and the truth and the life. No one comes to the Father except through me~ John 14:6.

The whips used were made of braided leather, with pottery shards and sharp stones affixed to the ends, which tore open the flesh of the prisoner with each cruel swing of the whip. When we picture this terrible, inhumane form of physical punishment we recoil in horror. Yet the physical pain and agony were not all Jesus suffered. He also had to undergo the mental anguish brought on by the wrath of His Father, who punished Him for the sinfulness of mankind—sin carried out despite God's repeated warnings, sin that Jesus willingly took upon Himself. He paid the total price for all our transgressions.

Under the guidance of the Holy Spirit, the apostle Peter wrote, "He Himself bore our sins in His body on the tree, so that we might die to sins and live for righteousness; by His wounds you have been healed." I am reminded that Isaiah 53 tells me that Jesus' future life on earth was foretold in the clearest of terms, to include his eventual torture and death. Being reminded that God was pierced in his side for our transgressions and he was crushed for our inequities, the punishment that brought us peace was upon God, and his wounds, (by his stripes) we are healed.

I began to remove anything or anyone that caused me or my body physical or mental stress. I expected God to heal me and I walked in my spiritual and physical healing every day. God made me his example, and he showed me plenty of miracles along my life's journey. I am forever grateful for all of my life experiences. When I look back over my life, and where God has brought me from, what he has done for me, where he has taken me to even this present day, I am overjoyed that God loves me that much. The covering that God has over my life, the divine protection, and the divine assignments keep me going. I am called to live in Gods purpose for my life. I have been called to a higher purpose and have been called to unapologetically go after my dreams and desires, despite what anyone may say or think about me.

Proverbs 3:5-6 ~Trust in the Lord with all your heart and lean not on your own understanding, but in all your ways, acknowledge him, and he shall direct your path. Words of wisdom that I share with people in my circle about my life journey is simple. Learn to love without condition. Most of all, care for people without any expectation and love them when they cannot love themselves. Be unapologetic for living your life the way you live, because your life is a gift, your journey is amazing, and you are responsible for creating a happy and fulfilling life. Be unapologetic for creating success in your life and surrounding yourself with individuals who are like-minded and headed in the same direction as you are. Keeping in mind that not every one that started on your life journey is designed to go to every level and every step with you. In this journey called life, we all have choices. We should all take chances to create a successful pathway for our journey in life and remember as long as you live you will experience some form of challenge. Challenges are what makes life interesting, and overcoming challenges is what makes life more meaningful. Lastly, listen to your heart, trust your instincts, know that you can do anything you put your mind and heart to. Dream it, dare it, and do not be afraid of it. Keep the faith and follow your vision, follow your passion. Anything is possible if you BELIEVE! **B**ecause **E**mmanuel **L**ives **I** **E**xpect **V**ictory **E**veryday!   That was a phrase that I heard at a woman's conference with my sister's church.

To be truly happy, it is important to have a clear sense of direction. Commit to something bigger than yourself that can bring you and others joy. In considering this recommendation, there will be a sense of God's will for your life. Your life will stand for something, and somehow you will begin to make significant contributions to your world. I also learned during times when my calling was not as clear to me, not to make assumptions. I found the courage to ask questions and tap into resources that could help me get to the next level in my journey. I communicated with others as clearly as I could, and with the support of many people in my corner, my life has been completely transformed.

I am a firm believer to whom much is given, much is required. I also believe that the past is the past. Continue to press forward and release yourself from any past hurt, pain, and disappointments. For the best is yet to come. Each day that I am blessed to wake up, I take that as a sign from God to live in the preset moment. As challenging as "living in the moment" can sometimes be for me, it provides me with a chance to start over, start fresh with each new day, each new hour, and each new minute.

I decided at the age of 3 that becoming successful was the only option for me. It was not always clear how I would reach that goal, but through prayer and asking for God's will to be over my life, I have accomplished a lot during my lifetime and I am looking forward to the next phase in my life to see where God takes me in the years to come. There have been many turning points during my lifetime and to achieve success has been part of my DNA. Trusting and believing in myself has not always been easy, but through self-help, self-awareness and activating my faith in God, it has become easier with time. While the path to our destination is not always a straight one, facing many detours or road blocks, the path to my success is my journey. The pathway to my success has allowed me to embark on many roads. As I continue down my pathway to success, and living in my pathway to purpose, I remain unapologetic for the success that I have achieved and for the success that I have created. Simply put, I am unapologetically me! I am thankful to God for choosing me to go down my distinct pathway to purpose and I would not trade it for the world!

ABOUT THE AUTHOR

Dr. Jacquelyn R. Jones is originally from Strongsville, OH, a suburb of Cleveland, OH. She is a first-generation college student, who went to The University of Akron to become an Akron Zip, where she obtained a Bachelor of Science degree in Sport and Exercise Science with a concentration in Sports Management. She graduated Cum Laude. She received a Master of Science degree in Higher Education Administration. Dr. Jones has her Doctorate of Philosophy degree in Higher Education Administration with a minor in Human Resource Management from The University of Toledo. Her published dissertation is entitled *College Self-Efficacy and Campus Climate Perceptions as Predictors of Academic Achievement in African American Males at Community Colleges in the State of Ohio.* Dr. Jones is the first in her family to receive a Ph.D. She is a professional with a motivating message of self-discovery and self-empowerment to all she encounters. She is a woman who is determined to succeed in life and believes in the scripture, "to whom much is given, much is required!"

Jacquelyn believes in the power of one person to make change. Jacquelyn is on a mission to change lives of young people through her work in higher education and in the community. Jacquelyn has worked at a variety of colleges and university campuses. Through her extensive work in higher education, she developed a passion for college access, student success, retention and completion. As a university administrator, Dr. Jones has been a vital decision maker who provides solutions to address problems or concerns in the higher education setting.

She has presented workshops at national, local, state and regional conferences on topics that include leadership development, trends in higher education, diversity issues in higher education, self-efficacy and campus climate of African American males and has published an article with other colleagues from The University of Maryland entitled *Examining Race and Leadership: Emerging Themes,* which appears in the higher education journal of Concepts and Connections.

Dr. Jones is an active member of Delta Sigma Theta Sorority, Incorporated and has previously served as a board member for the Martin Luther King Kitchen for the Poor. She was recognized as an honoree and Emerging Leader for the Toledo African American Legacy Project and is also a member of Rotary Club. Dr. Jones currently resides in Greensboro, North Carolina and works at The University of North Carolina at Greensboro.

JACQUELYN R. JONES, PH.D.

06

CHAPTER

06

THE ART OF PRACTICING PASSION

TAMI M. PRINCE, M.D.

THE ART OF PRACTICING PASSION

PART 1

Passion

[*Pash-un* n]

Noun

1. Any powerful or compelling emotion or feeling, as love or hate.

2. A strong or extravagant fondness, enthusiasm, or desire for anything.

3. The object of such a fondness or desire

4. Strong sexual desire; lust

Everyone has a story to tell. Mine is the story about passion. Passion is what one lives and breathes for unapologetically. Passion keeps you going and keeps you young hearted. Passion is what we were all put on this earth by God to do. You may ask what is my passion? What is that something that keeps me going and makes me happy? Well my "something" is the art of healing and helping others.

My parents taught me at an early age that I must have something that I wake up for and look forward to every single day. They encouraged me to strive for and break through the glass ceiling that was so elusive to many black Americans. They nurtured my fascination with science and medicine and told me that I can be whatever I wanted to be if I excelled in school, kept my eye on the prize, and was persistent. That encouragement also fueled my desire to be an attorney, teacher, and Dallas Cowboy Cheerleader. In the end, I found the field of medicine to be most fascinating and it allowed for me to help others in their time of need and advocate for those who are unable to speak for themselves.

PART 2

The catalyst for my decision to focus on a career in medicine was my maternal grandmother's health struggles. As a young child and teenager, I did not fully understand her struggles with mental illness, diabetes, and hypertension. My grandmother, like so many Americans, had to choose between eating and paying for her medications. Her medical insurance did not cover her medications which where hundreds of dollars per month. Therefore, she chose to eat. That choice came at a high cost and she subsequently died at an early age as the result of uncontrolled diabetes and hypertension. She died two days before my 16th birthday. My sweet 16 was spent mourning my grandmother's untimely death. I found myself asking "what if my grandmother was able to afford her medications, would she still be alive?" I vowed after her death that I would fight tooth and nail for my patients and ensure that they had of all the resources needed to help with obtaining their medications. I wanted to arm my patients with a wealth of knowledge so that they can have a healthy lifestyle and manage chronic illnesses so that they do not meet an untimely death as my grandmother did.

My path to becoming a physician has not been easy. The typical path to becoming a physician is to complete four years of college, four years of medical school, and several more years depending upon the specialty of medicine chosen. My path was slightly varied to say the least. I attended Spelman College and chose my major as biology on day one. Science majors were the hardest working women on campus and it was very difficult for us to graduate in four years unless we went to summer school and overloaded on credit hours. The maximum credit hours one could carry per semester was 18, and at one point, I was taking 21 hours just to graduate on time. I do not know how I would have survived if I did not have faith in God that He would not place more burden on me than I could handle. I tried hard to balance the rigors of being a biology major with having a social life. On more than one occasion my social life may have gotten the best of me and caused me to stumble with my academics but I have zero regrets. I made lifelong friends, pledged the illustrious Delta Sigma Theta Sorority, Inc., and graduated on time with a Bachelor of Science in Biology. This last part is a minor miracle as science majors historically had a hard time graduating on time. I always kept my eye on the prize with my motto being "failure is not an option." I even had that motto as my computer screensaver as a constant reminder that I must succeed. Even if I stumbled, I had to learn how to keep it moving forward. I was on a mission!! A black woman on a mission is something to rise and take note of.

After I graduated from Spelman College, I was burned out from school and hated my alma mater and Atlanta. I also did not get into my top medical school choice, which made me hate school even more. I wanted to go back home to Cleveland, Ohio and never return to the city where I began to shape my womanhood and career in medicine. When I decided to sit out of medical school, one of my sorority sisters gave me the best advice. She told me that while I was sitting out and trying to figure out if I still wanted to pursue my path to becoming a physician, I should work in a completely different field. If I still had the burning passion to become a physician while I was performing another job, then medicine was the right decision. I took that advice and began working for a Fortune 500 company. While I enjoyed my job, it did not light my fire in the way that medicine did. I did not yearn for my job the way that I yearned to practice medicine. I decided to reapply for medical school and this time I only applied to two schools in Ohio. I knew that I wanted to stay close to my family and that I did not want to waste the time and money applying to schools that I had no desire to attend. I also happened to hail from a state with the best medical schools and hospitals that are world-renowned. I took a gamble only applying to two schools but the gamble paid off and I was accepted to both schools. I subsequently chose Wright State University School of Medicine.

Wright State University was in a city that was much smaller than where I grew up or went to college. It was a great town as there were very little distractions, unlike Atlanta or even Cleveland for that matter. I buckled down and focused solely on my studies. I reveled in gross anatomy, histology, biochemistry, and all the other classes that we had to attend in the first two years. My grades in medical school were better than my grades in college, believe it or not. I think that my "gap year" was exactly what I needed and helped me to regain my focus. I was not interested in being in the "in crowd." I was only interested in excelling in school and graduating. I was strong-willed and my dream was finally within my grasp. My dream was mine for the taking and I was going to take it at all costs. I continued to excel in my clinical rotations during the last two years of school. It was during these rotations that I decided to become an Obstetrician and Gynecologist. I absolutely loved my Ob/Gyn rotation, which was ironic, as I had entered medical school with the mindset that I would become a Family Practitioner or Internist. I kept an open mind during all rotations and it allowed me to see other specialties in a different light. Ob/Gyn gave me the best of every aspect of medicine that I enjoyed. Ob/Gyn allowed for me to care for female patients from the reproductive years through menopause and beyond. It also allowed me to perform surgeries. Had I had a closed mind I would have never appreciated the diversity in Ob/Gyn. Now that I chose Obstetrics and Gynecology, I then had to choose which residency programs to apply. Once again, I decided against applying to umpteen programs knowing that I had no desire to train at those programs. I knew what I wanted and took another gamble. I applied to three programs and proceeded with the interview process. My decision came down to my home school's program and Riverside Regional Medical Center combined Ob/Gyn and Family Practice. I liked the latter as it combined my original desire to become a Family Practitioner with my passion for Ob/Gyn. I liked my home program as I was familiar with the residents and the attending physicians. I learned a great deal from them but in the end I chose the Riverside program as I was ready to spread my wings and leave Ohio once again. Ohio was home for me. Ohio was comfortable and safe. Ohio reinvigorated me to continue to pursue my ultimate passion. None of this was enough for me though. I wanted to experience even more and boy did I.

Nothing is quite as it seems. This was especially true once I got to Riverside Regional Medical Center. What was billed to me as a combined Ob/Gyn and Family Practice program ended up being a great pipe dream. Upon my arrival at my new program, I was told that the program chair was not going to be the person from which I was so eager to learn from but someone who I knew absolutely nothing about. To add more salt to the wounds, the entire Ob/Gyn staff made a mass exit. All that was left were three staff-attending physicians who ended up being subpar. This is not how I envisioned my intern year to begin! The saving graces were that we still had strong Maternal-Fetal Medicine and Family Practice staff attending physicians and private Ob/Gyn attending physicians. I tried to make the best of the situation as it was out of my control. I called on God to continue to provide me the strength to push forward. This was just another obstacle that I would have to overcome on my journey. I learned to use each obstacle that I encountered to my advantage. Obstacles are mere distractions designed by the devil to siphon your focus and plan. Obstacles have you concentrating on something on which you had no business concentrating. The silver lining in this unfortunate turn of events, is that much of what I learned in my intern year of residency I incorporate in my current practice. In the end, I decided to transfer to another program to complete my Obstetrics and Gynecology residency. My dream of being both an Ob/Gyn and Family Practitioner was over and I had to regroup immediately. I had to move quickly to find another program that had a second-year resident opening as it is much harder to change programs in the residency years without prolonging the four-year time. I saw an opening at The Ohio State University and jumped for joy. I was home sick by then and missed my family. Virginia was far and I could not go home as often as I did when I was three hours away in Dayton. I applied for the position, interviewed, and subsequently was offered the position.

The Ohio State University Medical Center Obstetrics and Gynecology program was very prestigious. It was also a very malignant program. This program's attending staff physicians were world-renowned and at the forefront of medical research. The Maternal-Fetal Medicine staff-attending physicians were the authors for the book from which all Obstetricians and Gynecologists in this country read and learn. Thankfully I had tough skin. Since I did not begin my residency at The Ohio State University, I was deemed an outsider. I was also only the fourth black woman to matriculate through this program.

Much of my learning from Riverside crossed over to Ohio State. My judgment was always questioned even if I was correct. As such, if it was not "The Ohio State" way of doing things, then it was no way. One resident even went to great lengths to try and ambush me in a Morbidity and Mortality meeting. Morbidity and Mortality, better known as M&M, was a way for physicians to present cases that may not have had great outcomes to learn from others. M&M was a grueling process as it was designed to dissect every single detail in the case. I was involved in a case my third year with an adverse outcome and was volun-told to present the case for M&M by this senior resident. Little did she know, I was several steps ahead and saw her coming before she saw herself. In the end, all the Maternal-Fetal Medicine staff-attending physicians defended me much to this resident's chagrin. During the M&M, she tried to question my decisions in the case, but she showed how weak her knowledge base was, and how strong mine was as I followed guidelines. Sometimes bad outcomes occur and no fault can be assigned as it may have been God's will for whatever reason. I am quite sure that her intent was not to show how smart I was, but that was the outcome of her vindictive behavior. God does not like ugly and rewards those who have faith in His abilities. I have always had strong faith. Faith is what has allowed me to survive and continue towards my goal of breaking the glass ceiling. My faith is what allowed me to graduate from The Ohio State University Medical Center Obstetrics and Gynecology Residency Program.

After residency, I decided that I wanted to return to Atlanta. I began to fall in love all over again with my alma mater, Spelman College, and the city of Atlanta. My time away helped me to appreciate all the valuable life lessons that I was taught during my four years in college. It also helped that the city was experiencing a rebirth due to the 1996 Summer Olympics. Atlanta was the place to be and I wanted to be a part of its rebirth. It was kind of my rebirth and evolution as well. What I did not know is how difficult my task would be trying to make my return. Many of the jobs catered towards Georgia native residents and those who trained in residency programs in Georgia. As I got turned down for jobs, I used the rejection as a catalyst to go against the grain and my diligence paid off. Or so I thought. I finally had my first job in Georgia.

My new job was about 45 minutes south of Atlanta. It was a very small town where everyone knew everyone. The residents always waved, said hello, and called me ma'am. I remember the very first time I was called ma'am by a patient I turned around because I thought my mother may have been standing behind me. See up north no one is ever addressed as sir or ma'am. Those titles were reserved for older people as a sign of respect. What I learned when I moved back down south is that everyone is addressed with these titles no matter how old you were. That was southern tradition and hospitality. My daddy always told me the south was different. This southern hospitality and niceties, however, could lull one into a dangerous comfort level where you drop your guard and never see the enemy coming. Southern hospitality, some say, is ultimately to blame for the final demise of my practice's operating and managing partner.

My managing and operating partner was a very accomplished Obstetrician and Gynecologist in this small town. He built his practice into one of the most successful practices in town. Everyone loved him as he was very charismatic. At first the other colleagues appeared to respect him but after a while their southern niceties turned to disdain. They hated the fact that he was more successful and that he was building his practice by hiring a diverse population of male and female physicians. They feared that if they did not shut him down soon that he would put them out of business. They began looking for cracks in his character and his art of practicing medicine. By now he had opened a second location and was able to duplicate his success. He began splitting his time between the two locations much to the disdain of the colleagues. They then used that against him and began the plot to force him out of our small town. My hospital privileges were blocked as they possibly saw that as an opportunity for him to step away even further from the practice. The hospital then convinced him to voluntarily give up his hospital privileges unless he uprooted his entire family and moved to town full-time. They had him right where they wanted him and I was stuck in the middle. He began to breach my contract and subsequently I decided to leave the practice effective immediately. Enough was enough! My first job out of residency was not what I ever envisioned and I was back at square one. Job search sucked but it was not long before I found another job. This new job would require me to move to Kentucky. It was goodbye to Atlanta and Georgia for a second time.

Now my time in small town Georgia was not all bad. I learned some valuable lessons about business, crafting my art of practicing medicine, and sadly racism. As a northerner, I had never witnessed racism first hand or I did not think so. I probably have been denied things without knowing it, due to the color of my skin and/or my gender, but I saw that as an opportunity to prove naysayers wrong. I am a person of action and I would much rather show you my capabilities than talk about them.

My daddy would always tell me about his life growing up as a black man in Birmingham, Alabama. Life was not kind to the black man in Alabama. He never wanted that life for his children, which was the reason he left Alabama and relocated to Cleveland, Ohio. My mommy was a Clevelander so she, too, never experienced racism in the way that my father did. My mother had all the beauty qualities that whites and blacks alike coveted. When I initially decided to attend Spelman, daddy gave me one of his "talks" about dealing with people in the south. This talk was crucial for so many reasons and even though I hated the talks at the time, I learned to appreciate my daddy and daughter time. My father just wanted to make sure that his little girl was aware, safe, and protected. He made sure that I never trusted anyone, even with their southern niceties. These talks allowed me to see right through the smoke and screen that my colleagues in Georgia had set in motion. It was too late for my former partner but not for me. It was time for me to soar to even greater heights even though obstacles continued. What does not kill you makes you stronger. Obstacles are mere distractions designed by the devil to siphon your focus and plan. Obstacles keep one concentrating on things upon which one has no business concentrating and thus never achieving the goal. Obstacles and the strength that I have gained maneuvering around them has allowed me to speak up, not only for myself, but for others who cannot speak for themselves.

After leaving Georgia, I decided to do locum tenens jobs with the military as an independent contractor. It afforded me the opportunity to travel and experience medicine in a different light. I was not tied down to one job indefinitely unless I wanted to stay. It kept my mind sharp as practicing medicine in the military is different than in the civilian world. Military medicine had its good and bad qualities just as practicing medicine in the civilian world. I liked that the patients were more compliant with medical care as the sponsor of the patient could be disciplined for non-compliance. The patients overall were very appreciative of the care that they received. I was outspoken when standard of care was not followed as this could adversely affect patient care. My patients meant everything to me. My patients depended on me to be their advocate. I had no problem fighting for them whatsoever. Of course, my outspokenness ruffled many feathers but I did not care. All I cared about was that my patients had the best outcomes. Even if that outspokenness was at my expense. These military people were not use to someone who was not afraid to speak. They were used to people being quiet and taking orders. I am quite sure that they thought "how dare this black civilian woman physician tell us what to do?" My contract was subsequently non-renewed but I was not mad in the least bit. I had made my mark as the ultimate patient advocate who dared to go against the grain for what was right. I would now set out to begin another journey… a business owner.

I love my rebirths. With every rebirth comes more wisdom, strength, and tougher skin. My faith in God also deepens. I have a sense of peace knowing that each decision made is what He wanted me to do. The lessons that I learn with each experience are the lessons that He wanted me to learn so that I can pass on those lessons to others. Throughout my journey, I have been able to pass on my lessons in the form of mentorship.

During medical school and residency, I was a participant in the Big Brothers Big Sisters program as a Big Sister to a high school young lady. Although her father was not present in the home, her mother and extended family were strong. They were a close family that always supported each other. They welcomed me into their families with open arms. Every Sunday after church, if I was not on call, I would go over to my little sister's grandmother's house for Sunday dinner. I loved to spend time with my little sister and she loved to spend time with me. One of my closest classmates in medical school also participated as a Big Brother to my little sister's best friend so we quite often would take both of our littles on outings together, which they loved. I lost track of my little sister after residency and she went to college. I guess we both got busy and life got in the way. I know in my heart that she is well as she had strong family support. My little sister's family was not the typical black, inner city, impoverished family with no father presence. She was not supposed to even qualify for the Big Brothers Big Sisters program. I think it was divine intervention that our paths crossed. My presence in her life helped her to see that black women can be anything that they want to be if they have faith, passion, and believe in themselves. Her presence in my life allowed me to pass on some wisdom but also allowed for me to press forward with my passion of helping others. It forced me to stay on top of my game as I realized that people looked up to me and I was a positive role model.

I have also been a mentor and speaker for Delta Sigma Theta Sorority, Inc., LaGrange, Georgia and Cleveland, Ohio Alumnae Chapters, as well as, career day guest speaker at Caledonia Elementary School in East Cleveland, Ohio, a mentor in Spelman College's Sister 2 Sister program and a mentor at Morehouse School of Medicine. I love mentoring as I love learning from and about my mentees. I love being able to pass on pearls of wisdom so that they have information that they may not hear anywhere else. My mentees also teach me more about myself and life in general.

Trying to become a solo practitioner was tough. A lot tougher than I ever expected. I entertained the idea of partnering with another physician but that never panned out. I decided to go it alone and then bring in another physician when I opened the practice. I financed my office space with money that I had saved and was all set to open my practice when my dream came to a screeching halt. The hospitals had begun to change their rules regarding board certification and number of cases that needed to be performed before extending privileges. While I was still board-eligible I was not certified in the time frame that had been set. As such I had to withdraw my application for one hospital that was near my office. When I researched the second hospital's rules and found that it did not have those requirements, I immediately began my application process for privileges. Sometime during my application process, winding through the channels the medical executive board decided to change their rules to match the other hospital. Once again, I did not meet the requirement for privileges and I withdrew my application. Should I have fought to be grandfathered in as my application was already in the process of review when rules changed? I strongly considered fighting. I had even hired two attorneys who charged top dollar for their time. Were they worth their high cost? I will reserve that judgment for another time. I prayed to God and had a long discussion with Him. I wanted to know if this was His dream or was it mine. If it was His dream, then I would continue to fight but if it was my dream then I would drop everything. I did not need to spend any more of my hard-earned money as I needed to come up with another game plan and quickly. After my long discussion with God, I realized that I was operating in Chronos and not Kairos time.

The concept of Kairos versus Chronos is very intriguing. It is a very important concept that one must understand to move forward in life. Kairos means "in God's time." Kairos is an appointed time or due season. Chronos, on the other hand, is chronological or sequential time. Most of us operate in Chronos as we define everything that we do based on the number of hours in a day. Ephesians 5:15-17 NRSV says *Be careful then how you live, not as unwise people but as wise, making the most of the time, because the days are evil. So do not be foolish, but understand what the will of the Lord is.* With this lesson that I learned from my many talks with God during this rough time in my life, I realized that I needed to reset my mindset to operate in Kairos. I realized that His dream was not for me to have my own business now. He had other plans for me and I needed to be ready for what He had in store for me.

Now most people would have been very discouraged by this point but not me. I am a different breed. I am a fighter. I am an advocate. I am a survivor. Once again, obstacles are tools used by the devil to knock you off your game. I used this disappointment to continue to reinvent myself. Once again, I gained even more wisdom, strength, and tougher skin that would propel me to my next level.

I became the Medical Coordinator for a substance abuse center in Atlanta, Georgia. This position allowed me to use my skills that I obtained while I attended medical school. My medical school had the Weekend Intervention Program, which was a program for people who were arrested on DUI or DWI charges, to rehabilitate themselves without going to jail. It was the first program of its kind in the country that was run by a medical school. As third year students, we could participate in the program. I liked the program so much that I became the first medical student at my school to become a certified substance abuse counselor. As a certified counselor, I could run group sessions. I was also the pathology lecturer for the program. My new position as Medical Coordinator allowed me to use my skills and it augmented my passion for helping people in their time of need. It allowed me to advocate for them when they could not speak for themselves. Addiction has such a powerful hold on people that it renders them too weak to fight. Clients/patients come to the substance abuse center when they have hit rock bottom and need help with rebuilding their lives sober. They are broken, homeless, and sometimes hopeless. This is right up my alley as I am the queen of rebuilding and rebranding. Clients are often in poor health when they arrive so I help them to regain health and strength. I coordinated and advocated medical care with health facilities that provided care to indigent patients, including mental health. I learned so much from these clients than I ever imagined. To be able to witness their evolution to sober living and rebuilding their lives pushed me harder to continue my evolution to practicing my passion.

I eventually did get my hospital privileges at a hospital in North Georgia. While I ultimately decided not to practice Obstetrics and Gynecology there, due to some unscrupulous business dealings that involved the owner of the hospital, the privileges opened more doors for me to be choosier about my opportunities, and not have to jump at the first job that came my way just because of the money. I needed to remain objective as there was more to life and the career than money. The privileges bought me more time so that I could sit still, open my ears, and continue to listen to God's plan for me. The Psalms are prayer requests for God and word of encouragement to God's people. God is all knowing so prayer is more for us than it is for Him. He already knows your prayer even before you do. God is still in control. Always. God is my refuge and strength. He fights for me and for you. Psalm 46:10 NRSV says *Be still, and know that I am God!* When I sat still God led me to my next opportunity.

This opportunity was a very unexpected twist that I had never considered. I was approached to work in an urgent care setting as a Gynecologist and Urgent Care physician. This urgent care liked surgeons and surgical subspecialists as we could perform many procedures that Generalists or Family Practitioners may not be able to perform. They knew that surgeons were fearless leaders and that trait was needed to run a busy center. They also wanted my Gynecology expertise as more women were coming to urgent care settings for Gynecologic issues. Most of this behavior was fueled by the trending climate in health insurance. I had never considered this opportunity because medical school only taught us traditional routes in medicine. Pick a specialty, attend residency in that specialty, and practice in that specialty indefinitely. Never did I hear about practicing medicine in an urgent care setting. This opportunity was different and intriguing. Could I make this work? Is this what I am supposed to be doing? Healing patients urgently versus over time? These were just a few questions that I had rolling around in my mind. God led me to this opportunity. I did not actively seek out this opportunity. I then began to believe that this was my calling so I accepted this offer.

I began my work in the urgent care setting. I found myself liking this setting of medical practice. It allowed me to use my knowledge base from my intern year at Riverside Regional Medical Center as a dual Ob/Gyn and Family Practice resident as well as my knowledge base from my Ob/Gyn residency training at The Ohio State University. I surprised myself with how much I remembered from my intern year and I continued to hone my skills. I was also able to keep up some of my minor surgical skills. I did miss Obstetrics, as well as performing major surgeries, but I had finally found my zone. I was afforded the opportunity to become a medical correspondent on Fox 5 News Atlanta Morning Show and Focus Atlanta CW69. The former segment was so well received in the Atlanta market that it aired in the Washington, D.C., Austin, Texas, and several other big Fox News markets. I was stunned, honored, and humbled that my segment spread to other markets in the country. For me to be able to reach so many people about important health topics was a true blessing. This job also provided me with the flexibility that I needed to partake in another passion... travel.

I love to travel and see the world. My passport is always ready to go on a new journey. I love to learn about other cultures and ways of life. I always tell people that I am a lifelong student. I can never learn too much. One can, however, learn too little and I did not want to be that person. Some people say ignorance is bliss. I say ignorance is just that. Ignorance. If one never traveled one would never learn to appreciate other cultures and races. My career has afforded me the opportunity to travel to five of seven continents. I am truly blessed that God has tapped me to experience things that others only can dream about experiencing. I have never taken for granted these experiences and opportunities.

Eventually I left the urgent care practice when I was being forced to practice outside of the scope of my training. That is a no-no in the medical field and I would not ever allow for anyone to compromise my principles and career. I had worked too hard to get to this point. I did not have a clear plan when I left my job but I was at peace with my decision to speak up. People asked me what my next move would be and I said that

God has not revealed it to me just yet. I once again sat still so that I could hear Him. When I sat still God led me once again to my current and best opportunity yet.

My current position is Medical Director for one of the largest Occupational Medicine companies in the country. Occupational Medicine was an area of medicine that was not mentioned in medical school. It involves caring for employees who have work-related injuries. Now one may ask themselves "why would an Ob/Gyn trained physician work in Occupational Medicine?" It is quite simple. Pregnant women, women of childbearing age, and menopausal women are employees that can have work-related injuries. Who best to take care of them than me? The field of Occupational Medicine is continuously evolving. There are so many dimensions to this specialty that I never become bored. I can use my honed skills and expertise to heal patients so that they can re-enter the workplace healthy. I often am the first to identify illnesses in these employees early that need to be further evaluated and treated by a primary care physician. I educate patients so that they either maintain their good health or restore and rehabilitate their health. I could not have asked for a better job than my current position. God dropped this job in my lap at the right time. Kairos time. I am always happy because I enjoy what I do. I now have a good work-social life balance. I have the flexibility to continue my other passion of traveling the world.

Will I stay in my current position? I hope not. I have so many opportunities with my company to advance so I hope to continue my advance to the next level within the company. This is my dream and I hope this will be God's dream for me as well. If not, I will go wherever He takes me. For now, I will enjoy the journey of practicing my passion.

ABOUT THE AUTHOR

Tami M. Prince, M.D was born and raised in Cleveland, Ohio. She holds a Bachelor of Science degree from Spelman College, the degree of Medical Doctor from Wright State University School of Medicine, and residency training in Obstetrics and Gynecology from The Ohio State University. Dr. Prince lives in Atlanta, Georgia where she serves as a supervisor, board member, mentor, public speaker, volunteer, television medical correspondent, and avid supporter of the arts and entertainment.

TAMI M. PRINCE, M.D.

07

CHAPTER

07

THE EVOLUTION OF ME

TERESA N. FOWLER M.D.

THE EVOLUTION OF ME

PART 1 WHO AM I?

For I know the thoughts that I think toward you, says the LORD, thoughts of peace and not of evil, to give you a future and a hope." Jeremiah 29:11

"I will praise You, for I am fearfully and wonderfully made, Marvelous are Your works, And that my soul knows well." Psalm 139:14

Who am I? That is really a hard question and I'm not even real sure if it is one that I can honestly answer, but let's take a journey and see if I can discover who I am.

My name is Teresa Nichole Fowler, M.D. and I was born on Friday August 21, 1970 to Mary Lee (nee Long) and Charles Otis Crews, Sr., the youngest of 5 children 2 sisters and 2 brothers. When I say I was the baby, I was the baby in every sense of the word. My closest sibling was 18 months older than me to the day and then after that there were 16, 17 and 20+ years between us. I always said my parents had multiple sets of children and they were old when they had me. Being the youngest girl was no fun either. Some people think that must have been the best and in some aspects it was but in others it was no fun at all.

I lived a very sheltered life from the minute I was born and treated very differently from my brother who was only a year older than me. My father was old school and didn't believe girls and boys should do the same things but I was a very stubborn and determined child. Everything my brother did I could do better and was determined to prove it too. I refused to be put into the stereotypical role of a girl … that was not who I wanted to be. Yes I was a girl and didn't really like to get dirty or have holes in my clothes or wear tennis shoes because my mother said they made your feet stink but I still was just as good and as valuable as any boy ever was. I had dreams and goals and they were going to come true no matter what.

I was a daddy's girl, spoiled rotten to the core in a good way I would like to think, but sometimes when I look back on it even though I don't like to admit it, I wasn't always very nice or lady like but in my eyes then it was ok. Whatever daddy said I could do or have, I did and had, and you better not say anything to me about it because I was going to say well my daddy said I could and you can't do anything about it. I know, not good. I hope I've gotten better over time but not real sure, just being honest.

I lived a very sheltered life oblivious of what was happening around me. I had for the most part everything I ever needed and wanted right at arms reach and if I didn't all I had to do was ask daddy for it. I might not get it right away but at some point rest assured it was a coming my way. I told you spoiled but that is how he kept me secluded and hidden away from the rest of the world and all the wonders and dangers of it.

Who I was, was tied up in my little world and all of the things in it but it still wasn't really helping to really understand who I was and how I fit into this world.

I went about my life as most children did, carefree and happy, not really understanding what was waiting ahead for me, but it was ok. Never did I think for one minute that it wouldn't be good.

The journey begins discovering who I am.

PART 2 THE EARLY YEARS

As I mentioned earlier I lived a very secluded life. My world involved my parents, my siblings and my nieces and nephews. You read that right. My nieces and nephews were pretty much the same age as my youngest brother and I, and they were more like my brothers and sisters when we were growing up, and I disliked them as much as I disliked my brother.

I spent a lot of time alone in my room or in some other part of the house just being me, whoever that was and I didn't like others in my space and could tell when my space had been invaded. Spending so much time alone is where I developed my own personal self and independence, not asking any one for help or for anything else for that matter. I came to prefer to be alone. Having to spend time with others became entirely too much work. Having to entertain and pretend to like being with them was becoming more and more difficult. In my time alone is also where I developed my love of reading and books. This is where my fascination for the world outside of my world began. The more time I spent alone, the more I couldn't wait to get out. But how was I going to get out? My daddy watched every move I made.

Education definitely was a priority in my house. The only reason I didn't go to school was if I were sick and then you better believe that if you didn't go to school you didn't do anything else either, so I quickly learned that would be the way I would explore the world. From the moment I stated school I never missed a day unless I was sick. I was pretty good at school too, and so was my brother, so now school became a competition as well. If he could do it I could definitely do it better. It seemed like I had all his teachers as well, and was constantly reminded of how great a student he was, so of course I had to outdo him, and I did and had to remind him of it always. I told you I was spoiled! As time passed I ended up with one friend who was in the same boat as I was. The youngest child, a girl and over protective parents, we became fast close friends. This friendship began in kindergarten and just continued to grow.

Life has a way of really challenging ones views of the world and people in it. As a child I depended on my parents for everything and nothing they told me could have ever been wrong because, of course, they were my first teachers, my first life lessons on trust and faith. If I couldn't trust or have faith in them then who would I ever be able to trust or have faith in, right?

Life continues and I am growing up and really learning that "hey, I'm one smart girl and didn't have to work to hard at it either." Now what was I going to do with it and how was I going to use my powers for good? I didn't know yet, but I knew it was going to be something good, no something great. For sure it was going to be better than my brother, no matter what it was because remember, anything he could do I could do better.

One day I decided I was going to be a pediatrician. I didn't know how to go about doing that but I just knew that is what I was going to do. So it was decided and there was no stopping me. I didn't have a plan B, or any other idea or thoughts of what else I could or wanted to be, as I was going to be a pediatrician. I made that decision maybe around the age of 7 or 8 and didn't look back. Of course I had those who said, "you're not going to be a doctor", and that was from my own family, and I would just say yes I am and didn't really pay what they said any attention because I could be whatever I wanted.

Life just continued and everything I did was with one goal in mind…to become a pediatrician. I knew I had to get good grades and go to school for a really long long time, but didn't know exactly what else I needed to do and didn't know who to ask about it. So I just kept saying this is what I am going be and that's all there is to it.

It really seemed like things couldn't move fast enough for me, and life became routine and involved a limited number of people, until one day my world was drastically interrupted.

After school one day, I was at home waiting on daddy to come home. I see the car pull in the driveway and he didn't get out, but my oldest sister did. Wait a minute! I didn't give her time to say anything. All I could remember asking was, "where is my daddy and why are you driving his car?" Daddy didn't let anyone drive his car and I immediately knew something was not right. Daddy had a heart attack and was in the hospital. That was the most terrifying thing ever. My daddy was not well, and not coming home. I can't see him…no that is not possible. He was my world and if I couldn't see him then the world was going to come to an end. It did end for almost 2 months. Time really stood still until I got to see him again. Daddy stayed in the hospital for almost 2 months and finally came home. That was the best day ever, but things would forever be changed. Daddy never worked again after that, at least not outside the house, so Momma did. When I look back on it now, it changed who he was as a man. Of course I didn't see that then. All I knew was that he was home and he wasn't going to work any more. He would be there everyday when I got home from school, which made me happy initially. I think that was really the end of my childhood innocence. The end of the early year of simple pleasures and just seeing the world and the people around me for what they were, just beautiful.

PART 3 THE DREAM BEGINS

Daddy did get better physically but he still didn't go back to work, and life just continued almost as if nothing had happened.

School became more of my get away because daddy was everywhere. Literally, he was everywhere. He walked me to the bus stop in the mornings. He was there when I got off the bus. Everywhere I wanted to go, he went, unless it was to school. I couldn't get a way from him. I couldn't breath. if I did my breath would have hit him. Talk about being sheltered, secluded and over protective, oh my all I could think was I couldn't wait to go to school tomorrow, grow up get out of this house, and I'm never going to treat my child or children like this.

Education was very important to my father. He never graduated from elementary school and was one generation removed from slavery, so it did mean a lot to him to make sure we were properly educated. As far as going beyond high school I don't think he really thought or cared much about that as long as we graduated from high school. He didn't even really care much about extra curricular activities. He would say you're not going to make any money doing any of that so just get your education.

I did just what daddy said. I went to school and studied hard and received outstanding grades, but after a while, that wasn't even enough for me. I had to get out of this house and the only way was to get involved in extra curricular activities. Even though daddy didn't really support that, as long as I kept my grades up, I could participate, and this was how I got out of the house without daddy's direct supervision.

Life is happening. I'm growing up, beginning to view the world and the people in it with rose colored glasses on, and most times was really not liking what I was seeing. I became defiant, lightweight disobedient skeptical about just about everything and everyone. It wasn't a pretty picture that was being painted from my view point but it really didn't matter to me much of what people thought or even what they thought of me for that matter. I had it all figured out anyway, you couldn't tell me anything. I knew who I was and what I wanted out of life and that I was going to get everything I had planned on. If you were in my way you better move or get ran over is how I felt.

I was very smart and had become quite a good athlete. I was a runner and was good. So I had it all together so I thought. I didn't have a lot of friends but didn't really need them because I had come to learn in my short, but yet very wise life, that people couldn't be trusted. They were eventually going to disappoint you and cause more anger and pain than I wanted to deal with or could handle. My job was to go to school and compete to the best of my ability, because in the end, I was going to be a pediatrician and no one else could do the work for me anyway.

I learned to speak life into myself and my situations early, even though I didn't know that is what I was doing until much later in life, but it was what kept me going. I also had my grandmother who encouraged me to be the best at whatever I was doing, and that I could and would, become whatever I set my mind on.

I did! I excelled at everything I did. I more than excelled and knew it. You couldn't tell me nothing. Now I knew I was smart and athletic but I did have other issues. I never really thought I was pretty enough, or even really loved either, because I didn't really hear it from my parents. I was very self-conscious about my appearance and my body. I felt as if I couldn't win for losing, something was always missing. I couldn't really put my finger on what that something was but just knew that something was missing. It was ok because I was going to become a pediatrician and that was all that really mattered anyway. I still didn't really know exactly how that was going to happen, just knew that it was going to become a reality. The journey through high school came and went like a flash of lightning. Now the real journey would begin. The pursuit of higher education. The means to an end, which was becoming a pediatrician. This was my life's dream and it wasn't going to stay a dream much longer.

PART 4 COLLEGE LIFE

College life, what an interesting concept. College life for me was about getting my education, get through these 4 years and move on to the next part of my journey. I wasn't interested in the party aspect of college. I wasn't even interested in making friends, because I had one plan to get this degree and go to medical school.

College was easy the first quarter, I got straight A's and was inducted into the Honor Society. I wasn't expecting anything less because I was a smart girl. That was what I did got good grades. Well that first quarter was a trick as things changed after that. I still did well but it wasn't the breeze I expected. I had to actually study a few times, read a couple books, and put in a little extra work, which was not at all what I was used to.

I started college with premed as my major not knowing that wasn't a major. I spent the first 2 years of my college career as a premed major until one day my college advisor burst my bubble and informs me that wasn't a real major, and I had to pick something else like chemistry or biology. Not really having anyone I could really talk to in order to get advice on what I should do and how to proceed, I just figured out what I needed to do in order to get out of there in 4 years, because I had a plan and it only consisted of college being 4 years. At the end of the day, I picked chemistry and got through it with decent grades, took a couple of bumps and bruises, and a set back or two but got out of there in 4 years just as the plan was to do.

Along the way I realized that I didn't really have everything completely planned out as maybe I should have. When I set out to be a pediatrician, I was 7-8 years old and just said, this is what I'm doing and that is it. I didn't have anyone to tell me how to exactly go about doing that. No one to keep me focused, or to help me choose the things that I needed in order to obtain the goal, which I had set for myself. I just knew I was going to be a pediatrician and I would figure it out as needed I guess. I thought I had things planned out. Graduate from high school, go to college as a premed major, finish in 4 years then go to medical school and finish in 4 years, as well and then on to residency. That was the plan and I had to stick to it.

I learned some valuable lessons between college and medical school. The main one being, I was as stubborn as they come and once I got an idea in my head there really was no changing my mind. No one was ever going to tell me I couldn't do something. I don't care who it was, what they said didn't matter. It only mattered what I said and what I wanted. At some point I learned the world didn't always work that way. The world didn't revolve around me anymore, it didn't revolve around my wants needs or desires. I was no longer living on my own personal island protected by the shark of all sharks, so I thought. I had to begin to adjust my way of thinking and how I was doing things but still the goal was to get what I wanted. I just had to make the world see that it really was going to happen.

Happen it did. Graduation from college was here. I had done what I needed to do to graduate in 4 years with my degree in chemistry, something I actually came to enjoy. It wasn't just a means to an end, and if I had to have a plan b I could be a chemist, but that wasn't the goal.

Graduation was especially important because was I not only the first of my siblings to graduate from college, but it was also my daddy's birthday. What a gift to be able to give him my college diploma. Even though I know now he was always proud of me, but I think this was a moment he was even more so delighted in my accomplishments because it was a celebration of celebrations, one that we would all remember until the next one that is.

PART 5 CATCH ME IF YOU CAN

I finally make it to that place where I have been trying to get to all of my life, medical school, I have arrived now. I can breathe a small sigh of relief right, its only just beginning.

I enter medical school on a longer track than what I had planned. Instead of a 4-year program it had turned into a 5-year program. It's okay because the end goal will still be the same. I will graduate from medical school with those 2 little letters that I had dreamed so long of, so who cares if its 5 years verses 4, I for sure didn't. It wasn't going to be as easy as I had anticipated or expected it to be, but I wasn't really sure what I expected, seeing how I really didn't have any real information as to what it would be. All I knew was that I was going to be a pediatrician and take care of the little ones no matter what the cost. I began to realize it was a cost that I had not fully calculated.

Medical school, my long awaited destination, had begun and the first day of class there I sat with my other classmates, the class of 1998, or so I thought boy was I wrong. On that first day, I am sitting in class like, what are these words they are saying and writing on the board and erasing faster than I could copy down? Oh is that what that medical dictionary was for? I spent more time trying to figure out what the word was and how to spell it before I could even begin to study it and how it related to what was being discussed in class. I was smart, why couldn't I understand what was going on? Why couldn't I keep up? I quickly realized everyone here was smart. Of course they were. You had to be to get in, but this was crazy. I felt as if I was taking a foreign language, being taught by a professor who came from a different country than even the language that was being taught. Now what was I to do? This was my dream right, to become a doctor. Not just any doctor, but a pediatrician, right? But first I had to master the language. I just had to, I couldn't quit now. I could not go back home and have everyone say, I told you that you weren't going to be a doctor, so the struggle became so real. It's okay, watch me do what I do, catch me if you can.

I took notes and bought a pocket tape recorder, so that way if I missed something, I could listen to the tape later, write it down and study it later and that way I wouldn't miss anything. That was easier said than done. The schedule was grueling, tedious, boring and down right difficult and I couldn't understand why that was. I was doing everything I thought I should be doing and besides this is what I wanted and I wasn't going to quit no matter how discouraging it may seem. Day after day, night after night, I gave it all I had and then some and still it was as if I was not doing well. What was a 5 year program turned into a 6 year program, and it was still okay, because I was still going to become the doctor I had planned and said I would be. There was nothing else. I didn't have a plan B in case this didn't work or go as I had planned. There was no need for a plan B when plan A was all I needed. It was all I ever had planned for and needed so I grit my teeth and carried on.

Set back after set back. Things seemed more and more discouraging. It just didn't seem as if things were going to get any better. It didn't seem as if my plans or my dreams were going to come to fruition, but what was I going to do because there was no plan B.

I was sitting in my kitchen one day, studying for a test that I had to pass, or I was going to get kicked out of medical school, and I was so desperate that I began to cry Lord please help me. You know what I need. I need to pass this test or they are going to kick me out. I can't get kicked out because this is where I'm supposed to be. This is my plan. I am going to be a pediatrician so I need your help to pass this test. This was the first time in I have no idea how long it had been since I talked to God. Which was so crazy because I was born and raised in the church. Seventh day Adventist church, at that, which in my circles meant something, so why had I not used what I was raised on, faith and trust that God would see me through? I didn't because I didn't really have my own relationship with God. I had my mothers and my sisters relationship and that wasn't nearly enough. I also had a grandmother who had prayed for me and given me something specific to read in times of trouble Psalm 27. That was my chapter specific for me that she had said when you don't know what else to do read that. So I cried some more and read even though I didn't understand it but I read and re-read it over and over and over again until I had it memorized. I didn't study my medical books, I studied my bible and I had a sense of peace and calm that it would be alright. Didn't really know that it would be alright, something just said to me trust Me. I took the test and I passed it. More than passed it, I got a flat out "A". I started crying all over again and I heard a voice say to me now why are you crying? Didn't you ask me for this? Didn't you say you needed this and that there was no plan B, it was plan A or else? Well here it is, I gave it to you because you asked me for it and you're still crying! Oh my that changed me and all I could say was you're right God I did ask you and it happened. I didn't have a plan B. I never understood why I didn't have a plan B but I knew I didn't need one. It became obvious that I didn't need a plan B because God was my plan A all along. Becoming a doctor wasn't the plan at all. The plan was developing a relationship with Christ and trusting in His plans not my own.

Now that was my very first personal experience with God, and I wish I could say that it was all it took for me to learn to depend on Him, first and foremost, but it was not. Although I knew that it was not by my own strength that I got through that test, and many more to come, it still was a long time after that before I truly knew that I could trust God with my everything.

After that experience it was really a race to the finish line. I knew I was on the right path to obtaining my goal and that I wouldn't be left. I didn't need a plan B but it was still an uphill war. Struggles that I had never planned to encounter of all sorts. Struggling trying to figure out still why are these things happening to me and why can it not be easier. But it was okay. I was determined to press on knowing that nothing worth having was easy, or not worth fighting for, so catch me if you can, no plan B here.

PART 6 LIFE IS HAPPENING

Life is already happening right? Life beginnings from the moment you take your first breath, right? Does it really begin there or does it begin at some other point? Well for me, of course, life started long before I thought it was happening but I just didn't realize it until it started happening to me.

Life was good, I was beginning to live out my dream starting to see the end of that long rainbow. Graduation from medical school was finally near. It had been a long difficult journey but it was finally nearing an end. At least that part of my journey anyway. Graduation day is fast approaching but I have no residency program to go to. What, wait a minute this is not supposed to be happening. Once medical school is over I'm supposed to go to residency, right? At least that is what I thought but I didn't. Life started happening to me. I found myself without a place in this continuing journey and I was heart broken to say the least. Okay, no problem, I'll just reapply next year. It's just that simple, but nothing up to this point was that simple. I thought I would have learned that by now but obviously not. What would I do with my year off? I had no idea so I just had to wait. I waited but not very patiently. The year came and went and it was time to reapply and the same thing happened, no place for me to go again now what? Well, a few telephone interviews and prayerfully a spot that was meant for me would come. Grand Rapids, MI here I come for the next step in my journey to reach a goal that I had set for myself a long time ago. Life begins to happen very quickly. New job, new city, new responsibilities. Now life really starts happening to me.

Let me see if I can explain it like this;

- 1998 House catches on fire.

- 1999 Graduation from medical school

- 2000 Residency begins

  *Mommas first encounter with breast cancer

  *My scare with potential breast cancer

- 2002 Going to the chapel and we're gonna get married

- 2003 Bundle of Jordan Nichole makes her appearance into the world

  *Completion of residency, time to go home.

- 2004 Separated, baby 18 months old. No job, no money, nothing!

- 2005 I get my first "real" job practicing medicine

  *Jordan and I are on our own

  *Mommas cancer comes back-radical mastectomy

  *Jordan starts preschool

- 2006 Daddy gets sick

  *Divorce is final

- 2007 Gramps dies

  *New job, finally only seeing children

- 2008 Daddy dies

  *Jordan and I move back in with momma

  *Jordan is 5, wow!

So see as I said, life is happening to me! I found myself in a place of great sadness and disbelief that this was actually my life. This was not supposed to be my life! Life kept happening, one thing after another, after another. As life was happening to me, I never really got to grieve the loss of the thing that had just happened, and because of that I ended up gaining about 30 lbs. I ended up on multiple blood pressure medications and an antidepressant, but life kept happening and I had to find a way to deal with it. I covered it well but sorrow consumed me and all I could say was, this was not supposed to be my life. How could this be the life that I dreamed about? It's not the life I dreamed about, why me? Why is this happening to me? The only good thing I saw about all of this, was the life that was given to me to take care of, to nurture, and to love Jordan Nichole. She had become my life, my source of happiness. Everything became about Jordan Nichole. The world revolved around her. I had to make sure I was doing everything I could do to make sure she had all she needed and wanted and more. There was nothing I didn't do for her, trying to ensure she didn't experience the pain of disappointment, loss, discouragement and grief. That became my life and a miserable life it was. Don't get me wrong, there still isn't anything I won't do or wouldn't have done for Jordan Nichole, but there was still something missing, and remember this wasn't supposed to be my life.

PART 7 LIFE GOES ON

Remember this isn't supposed to be my life, divorced single mother, semi-orphan living at home with my mother. The reality is that this was my life, and I had to get over it and find a way to deal with it, come hell or high water, it was what it was and the world didn't stop because this wasn't supposed to be my life!

Okay now what? Now that this is my life, what am I supposed to do? I have no clue. That was an issue for me because I always had a plan on what was to happen and how it was to happen. I had come to realize my plans weren't always the best. No matter how well intentioned or thought out I may have thought they were they never, I do mean never, came out the way I had planned. Life continued to happen all around me. Things changed but yet seemed to stay the same. How could that be? This was so confusing. This was not supposed to be my life. When are things going to change? When are they going to get better? I just need to not struggle so much, to not be so sad, and to just have somebody tell me it's going to be okay.

Well I have to keep moving, things will eventually get better, at least I hoped so. I really needed help, help with everything, and I had no idea where the help was going to come from, or even how to go about asking for it. I had never really had to ask for help before in my life and when I did I always asked my daddy, but now I didn't have him to ask any more. Life was hard and sad to say the least. Every consistent and good thing, the things I considered consistent and good in my life, had changed. They had disappeared. No one in my corner any more. No one rooting for me to succeed. It was hard. I found myself talking to myself a lot and to my grandmother often now. It seemed as if she knew exactly when to call me or when I would call her, she would say I was just thinking about you. I would go to the mailbox and find a letter from her with an encouraging word in it and a little something extra, which always brought tears to my eyes, how did she know.

Little by little things started to change, yeah sure life was still happening to me, and around me, but I was handling it a little better so I thought. When life happens to you and you don't have time to think about what is really happening, and no time to properly plan for it, things change but they remain the same at the same time. I had experienced so much loss, grief and sadness that I had no time to recover from any one event before the next one happened, but that's life right? It is but it isn't either. There never seems to be any peace or joy when that happens and I continued to find myself saying this isn't supposed to be my life and why is it continuing to happen this way? When is it going to be my turn to have some peace and some joy? I'm not asking for too much am I? All I want is just a little peace and happiness for myself, I think I'm entitled to it.

Now life has become routine. I get up in the morning, do what I need to do, get Jordan Nichole up and ready for school. Drop her off and I go to work. Work all day frustrated with my colleagues, with the work space, with my staff, my patients and my parents. I deal with it and leave work to now have to come home to my real full time job, being Jordan's mommy. That was, and still is, the most difficult job I have or will ever have, because if I can't manage my own life, how am I supposed to manage hers? Why didn't she come with a manual? After working all day and giving so much of me to my job, sometimes I felt as if I didn't have enough left for her, and of course I didn't want her to feel as if I valued my job over her. That was far from the case, but I had to provide for her financially. I had to make sure she had everything she needed and wanted. That was my job and I loved her more than my own life...she was my life.

Day after day, things went on, I guess, as they were supposed to. The routine of what I had put in place, in order to bring about some kind of order to the chaos that was taking place in my mind, continued as usual. If for any reason the routine was thrown off, my whole day was thrown off, and the chaos just intensified and I became a not so very nice person in general. Because I needed and craved for some kind of normalcy to make sense of the chaos, there had to be routine and order no matter what was happening around me. I'm sure to most people I appeared as if I had it all together when in reality I was screaming for help and wasn't being heard. I had become a professional at dressing up a mess! It seemed as if everyone else around me had it all together and I was the only one struggling with this thing called life. Nothing made sense to me, I had begun to wear a mask of happiness. I was good at playing the game! I had become very impatient and intolerant of things that I deemed had little importance to me or that I didn't think had anything to do with me. I barely had enough time and energy for my own life and for sure I didn't have time for yours. Yes, at work that was my job to listen and deal with and solve every one else's problems and concerns but I had become so cynical about life and people. I saw it as no one really cared about me, they just wanted something from me. I played the game well, did what I had to do, but the minute I would leave their presence, a spirit of contempt and anger would just come over me. When I would leave the office for the day, I didn't want to hear about anyone else's problems or see anyone else's child. I had my own problems and my own child that I had to muster up some strength to deal with. At the end of the day, I had just enough for the one who brought me joy, Jordan Nichole. She truly was my sunshine. But life goes on.

PART 8 REALITY CHECK

Again, this is not supposed to be my life. Lord why is this happening? This is not supposed to be my life!

One day I hear a voice say to me after for the millionth time I say Lord this is not supposed to be my life, why isn't this supposed to be your life? If it's not supposed to be your life then whose life is it supposed to be? Wait a minute, there was no one else in the room but me and I know that wasn't my voice. I paid it no attention and I hear the voice say again, whose life is it supposed to be if it's not yours? Okay, I'm game, because at this point I realize the Lord is answering my question and I say okay Lord, it is my life but it's not supposed to be like this. Why is it like this? God says to me, I never told you it was going to be easy and haven't I given you everything you've asked me for?

Now this isn't funny anymore. At this point I just begin to reflect, to really reflect on my life and EVERYTHING that has happened in my life, and realize that yes I have gotten everything I've asked for, but Lord I didn't ask for all the pain and heartache. Why not just leave some of that out? Was it really necessary? I didn't get an answer, well at least not right away.

As life continued to happen to me and around me, every time I would begin to say this is not supposed to be my life, I would hear God say why not? There would be times when I would just say okay Lord, I don't have time for this and other times I would say, because it's not supposed to be. I don't like it like this it's too hard and I just can't deal with it. I don't want to deal with it. It's not fair this life right here is not fair. I really didn't ask for this. Life continued to happen and little by little, it didn't always seem so difficult and I began to enjoy some of the things I used to. I didn't question what it was, I just prayed that it would continue. Things started happening in my life that were unexplainable. People were put in place to help with the hardships of life where I didn't feel alone any more. There just was a peace about life, no matter what was coming my way, it was ok. The sun started shining a little more. It would be brighter on some days than others and stayed around longer. Even on those days when the sun wasn't as apparent, I wasn't as discouraged as before. I began to read again, not just anything or everything, but my Bible and studying it more and more. That had to happen because Jordan Nichole was in a Christian school and environment and she began to question everything and sometimes the only answer I could come up with is because God said so, but couldn't go beyond that. At first, that was enough for her, but of course after a while it was, but why mommy why, and I had to be able to give her a better answer. It was hard, very hard, because every word I read, it seemed as if everything I had been questioning about life was being answered right there, and that God was speaking directly to me and most times I didn't really like it. The truth was hard to see, hear and accept, especially when I had been wallowing in my own sorrow for so long and the truth had been there all a long.

Reality began to hit up side my head, in my face, on my hand and every other available space it could, and it was a hard pill to swallow. The reality was I had gotten everything I asked for but some where a long the journey I forgot that nowhere did I ever say, make it easy. Even if I did, I believe that it still wouldn't have been easy but maybe if I had of started with the right person from the start it would have been easier to bear. God placed people in my life, whether for a short or long time, for good or bad that fed into my spirit and into the person that I am today.

I truly began to realize to whom I belonged as more and more people began to sow good seeds into my life and how valuable I really was and now I could see life through a different set of glasses. I could appreciate where I had been and what I had been through that there really was a purpose for my pain and my failures not just my happiness and successes. For everything that had happened in my life whether good bad or otherwise, was to develop me into the person that I am so that I could truly realize where my real help came from.

Trust and believe that it has not been an easy journey, or even one that I really wanted to take, and it is still far from over. There are times when it is still very difficult but because of a renewed love, it is easier to travel this journey of life. I have learned to accept who I am, flaws and all, and to look at my own life and situation and ask for help from the only one who can truly give me all I have ever needed and wanted before I can even begin to give to anyone else. Now not to say I am so consumed with me and mine only, but because I don't have to be so worried about who is going to take care of me and provide what I need and want knowing that that has already been taken care of, I can really focus on what my real purpose is, and that is really to tell others about my story which involves how incredibly good God has been to me. What I have found is that when I am being a blessing to others they are really blessing me. How incredible is that!

Reality is and was that life was not really about me and my little issues in life. Everything I had been through Jesus had already been through, and had planned a way for me to go through what He knew I was going to go through. The truth is life is going to happen. The reality is how am I going to handle it?

PART 9 LIFE BEGINS AGAIN

Now life has begun again. No, not death and rebirth, at least not in the physical sense but in the emotional and spiritual sense.

Each new day begins another opportunity to continue on this journey of life. Another opportunity to contribute in some way shape, form, and fashion to sow good seeds for the change that I want to see. Another opportunity to start a new page of another chapter to tell the story that only I can tell.

My life has been filled with many ups and downs, successes and failures but through it all I finally can see some of the reason behind it. Not only do I have another opportunity to attempt to get it right, but to be a blessing and be blessed by all of those in my life, be it for a season or a lifetime. Sometimes we don't get multiple opportunities at happiness, now I said happiness, not joy there is a difference, but I've had the opportunity many times to have happiness and to bring others happiness.

I'm trying to figure out what my purpose and my passion is and then what am I supposed to do with it when I find it? Things that I used to see as a chore and draining has really turned into my passion and it really has always been my passion. I am a pediatrician by profession but my passion is for children. I know that sounds like the same thing but it really isn't. There is something so wonderfully beautiful about a child, their innocence and simple way of looking at life and not taking anything for granted. Their utter dependence on those who are supposed to take care of and love them and then just what they give back to you. Most times children simply want to be loved and give love in return and it is so beautiful and heart warming.

I just can't even begin to put into words really the meaning to just see things from a child's point of view and to just take it for what it is. I love them and in turn have the opportunity to sow into their lives not knowing the entire time they were sowing into mine. It's amazing how God works like that. Not only did he give me the profession I asked for, but he gave me much more than I could have ever realized.

I have an amazing little girl who isn't such a little girl any more. Jordan Nichole is turning into the young lady God has called her to be and I am honored to have been chosen to be her mother. When I think I am leading her, she is leading me. I am in total awe of her, she has no idea and if she did she would just say I am embarrassing her. For a long time I had bought into the reality that it would just be me and her at least until she turned 18 and then it didn't really matter. Everyone that I had met just wasn't right. It was something about them that didn't match up any more to who I was and what I knew I deserved and I wasn't going to settle again. I was entitled to better to the best. During the time of just Jordan Nichole and I, I had to do some self-reflection and introspection as to what was it about me that wasn't ready to receive what I felt I deserved. I began to get real specific with God about what I wanted in a man, a life partner, a protector, the man my child was going to spend most of her time with. He couldn't just be anybody, I had already done that, been there too, too many times and refused to do it again. I really just figured it wasn't meant to be and I was going to be single for the rest of my life. My sister would tell me I was being picky and wasn't making myself available, but I had requirements. I was at a point in my life where I didn't want to have to "train" somebody on what to do and how to do it. He needed to know how to do that already. So I got specific with God. I need a man who loves

176

God more than he loves me. I needed him to be taller than me with my 4-inch heels on. I needed him to be "the man" already. Is that wrong of me, I didn't think so. But apparently I wasn't ready for him yet, God was still working on me, which was fine. God had to let me see that even if he allowed me to get married again, that no matter what He was really all I ever truly needed and that He had always been here with me. He had never left me even when I thought He had, He was my true source of joy. If I had joy in Him it didn't matter what my emotional state was that particular day, I still could have joy. What an amazing truth.

Over time I found more and more joy and peace and was very comfortable just being me. Really being me and it was okay and that's when God brought me an amazing man. The man He had created initially just for me, and had I only waited to begin with, I would have spared myself much heartache and pain but again if that had of happened, I wouldn't have been ready for him.

Life really did begin again, new husband, new job, new place to live, a new outlook on life. A freshness that I had never experienced before. Now it wasn't easy at first because at this time it has just been Jordan Nichole and I for so long that I was her world and she was mine, so it took us both some time to adjust and for her to understand that Chief wasn't here to take me away from her or replace her in anyway but to add to not just my life but hers as well. To add life in a way that neither one of us had ever really known.

Although God had already made it clear that by no means was I ever alone and I always had help when needed, but now I had someone else to help bear some of the burden of my daily routine to support me when there seemed to be no support to be found, and I am grateful and life has truly gotten better. I didn't say easier, I said better from that stand point.

I also realize that at times I lose sight of the giver of gifts and focus on the gift more than I should and from time to time I need to be reminded. This is currently one of those times. My nature is to care for people, to be the support when there is none, to do when no one else will, but I find myself with the shoe on the other foot. I currently have vertigo that is where everything around you is spinning. I have been suffering with this for many months now and again like all other times, find myself saying why Lord? This is not supposed to be my life. I am supposed to be taking care of others not them taking care of me. I am in a time of transition of what is going to happen in my life and as usual I make all these plans and of course they never play out the way I say they should and you would have thought I would have learned my lesson by now but obviously not at least in all areas. Anyway it is obvious I have over looked the giver of the gift and am more focused on the gift again and the gift-giver has said I need you to sit down and be still so you can hear what I am saying to you and telling you what to do not you telling me what you are going to do. I am trying to be patient but it isn't working I'm tired of sitting around the house not driving myself where I want to go, doing what I want when and how I want not going to work and helping those who I was called to help, but He says you still haven't learned your lesson. Yes my plans may have what I consider to be pure motives but they aren't Gods plans and so right now I am sitting trying to be patient to let God lead and guide me and to not lose focus of the gift-giver as life is beginning again.

PART 10 WHO I AM

I started out with "Who am I" and here I am with "Who I Am." Isn't that the same thing just stated a different way? Well let's find out.

Definitely my life has evolved over these last 46 almost 47 years, drastically changing at an almost alarming rate and I went from really questioning who I was and trying to figure out who that was and where I fit in this world? What is my purpose? My passion? My calling? Finally I can say with certainty, who I am.

I am a child of the most High God who is entitled to everything He says is mine! I am amazing, beautiful, caring, diligent, energetic, faithful, generous, headstrong, intelligent, joyful, kind, loyal, magnificent, nosy, optimistic, persistent/passionate/professional, quiet, resilient/respectful, strong, thoughtful, unmovable, vibrant, wise, exhilarating, youthful and zealous. I read something that said "Life is not a destination, it is a journey", and I never really understood what that meant until now. Sometimes I think that life and this journey of life is about one thing at a time when in reality its about the sum of the parts. That I've missed a lot of life just looking at one thing at a time and not really seeing the entire picture. I am learning to appreciate the entire picture. To just look at it for what it is and not dissect every little thing in it apart just in order to put it back again. Life is a continuous learning journey that never stops. I am in awe of the journey God has me on and all that He has for me and I am ready for all of it!

I love the me that I have become and still growing it.

I am striving to completely and wholly be the Proverbs 31 Woman:

Who can find a virtuous wife?
For her worth is far above rubies.
The heart of her husband safely trusts her;
So he will have no lack of gain.
She does him good and not evil
All the days of her life.
She seeks wool and flax,
She brings her food from afar.
She also rise while it is yet night,
And provides food for her household,
And a portion for her maidservants.
She considers a field and buys it;
From her profits she plants a vineyard.
She girds herself with strength,
And strengthens her arms.
She perceives that her merchandise is good,
And her lamp does not go out by night.
She stretches out her hands to the distaff,
And her hand holds the spindle.
She extends her hand to the poor,
Yes, she reaches out her hands to the needy.
She is not afraid of snow for her household,
For all her household is clothed with scarlet,
She makes tapestry for herself;
Her clothing is fine linen and purple.
Her husband is known in the gates,

When he sits among the elders of the land.

She makes linen garments and sells them,

And supplies sashes for the merchants.

Strength and honor are her clothing;

She shall rejoice in time to come.

She opens her mouth with wisdom,

And her tongue is law of kindness.

She watches over the ways of her household,

And does not eat the bread of idleness.

Her children rise up and call her blessed;

Her husband also, and he praises her:

"Many daughters have done well,

But you excel them all."

Charm is deceitful and beauty is passing,

But a woman who fears the Lord, she shall be praised.

Give her of the fruit of her hands,

And let her own works praise her in the gates.

ABOUT THE AUTHOR

Dr. Teresa Nichole Fowler, M.D. born and raised in Cleveland, OH. Married to her wonderful husband Dorian with 2 beautiful daughters Tatiana and Jordan. Currently living in Cleveland, OH practicing pediatrics at Cleveland Clinic Foundation. Attends Grace Community Seventh Day Adventist Church. Dr. Fowler is committed to being used by God and doing His will to help those whom He has called her to help and encouraging all women to become the woman God has designed them to be.

TERESA N. FOWLER, M.D.

Grace Roberts

A PRODUCT OF
KRYSTAL KLEAR COMMUNICATIONS, L.L.C.

This collection of short stories is a collaborative effort from 7 women across the county with one common thread, the CEO of Krystal Klear Communications, L.L.C., Audra T. Jones remarked as the "Krystal Klear Specialist"

Krystal Klear Communications is a firm with experience working with leading organizations, across the private, public, and social sectors, establish their niche and ultimately their brand. The firm provides strategic communications counsel to individuals, business owners and industry leaders who are interested in growing and protecting the value of their reputations and the value of their companies through brand awareness.

They help organizations align communications initiatives with business strategy; integrate corporate and marketing communications to achieve business results more efficiently; analyze and design the structure of organizations; and use communication to achieve organization objectives in times of triumph or challenge.

Krystal Klear Communications, L.L.C.

www.krystalklearexperience.com

Cleveland, Ohio

216.387.0375

info@krystalklearexperience.com

Social Media @ krystalklearex

Made in the USA
Middletown, DE
11 October 2022

12511791R00104